Holy Spirit, Th
Demons by Past

lent and the ma~~~~~~~~~~~~~~~~~~~~~~~~~~~~~~~~~~~~ teaching on the ministry of deliverance. "For this purpose the Son of God was manifested, that he might destroy the works of the devil" (1 John 3:8). It is powerfully compiled, worthy of study, and will give the reader insight on the ministry of deliverance that will open their eyes to the work of the Holy Spirit and power of the name of Jesus to set the captives free. I believe it to be a study manual filled with deliverance insight that will set many free and teach the reader to understand how the power of the Holy Spirit and name of Jesus work to destroy the works of the devil. It is an excellent study to read and go forth and set the captives free.

—APOSTLE IVORY HOPKINS
PILGRIMS' MINISTRY OF DELIVERANCE
GEORGETOWN, DE

Lereatha Gunnels-Mayberry
Mark 11:24-25

Holy Spirit

THE

DELIVERER

LOREATHA
GUNNELS-MAYBERRY

Holy
Spirit
THE
DELIVERER

CREATION
HOUSE

HOLY SPIRIT, THE DELIVERER: EVICTING THE DEVIL AND
HIS DEMONS by Loreatha Gunnels-Mayberry
Published by Creation House
A Charisma Media Company
600 Rinehart Road
Lake Mary, Florida 32746
www.charismamedia.com

Unless otherwise noted, all Scripture quotations are from the
King James Version of the Bible.

Scripture quotations marked NIV are from the Holy Bible,
New International Version. Copyright © 1973, 1978, 1984,
2010, 2011, International Bible Society. Used by permission.

Scripture quotations marked NAS are from the New
American Standard Bible–Updated Edition, Copyright ©
1960, 1962, 1963, 1968, 1971, 1972, 1973, 1975, 1977, 1995
by The Lockman Foundation. Used by permission. (www.
Lockman.org)

English definitions are derived from *Webster's New American
Dictionary*, by Merriam-Webster, Inc., New York: Smithmark,
1995.

Greek definitions are derived from *Strong's Exhaustive
Concordance of the Bible*, ed. James Strong, Nashville, TN:
Thomas Nelson Publishers, 1997.

Names of those receiving ministry have been changed.

Design Director: Justin Evans
Cover design by Lisa Cox

Library of Congress CataloginginPublication Data:
2014910812
International Standard Book Number: 978-1-62136-772-7
E-book International Standard Book Number:
978-1-62136-773-4

While the author has made every effort to provide accurate telephone numbers and Internet addresses at the time of publication, neither the publisher nor the author assumes any responsibility for errors or for changes that occur after publication.

First edition

14 15 16 17 18 — 987654321
Printed in the United States of America

DEDICATION

I dedicate this book, *Holy Spirit, The Deliverer: Evicting the Devil and His Demons,* to my parents, Matthew Herbert and Minnie Geneva Gunnels, who spent most of their lives in Conway County, Arkansas, and struggled through sharecropping, racism, and much more.

It is also dedicated to my husband, Melvin Mayberry; to my siblings Mae Ella Scott and O'Nella Geneva Kindle; and to my deceased siblings Marzetta Sheppard, Mattie Lee Gunnels, Sherman Gunnels, Daniel Webster Gunnels, Leroy Herbert Gunnels, Lillie Mae Dorris, and Leola Gunnels.

CONTENTS

PREFACE

HIS IS MY first book about demonology. Knowledge on deliverance has begun to increase. First we had to come to a place where we realized that Jesus cast demons out of believers as well as unbelievers and that Christians can have demons or be carriers of demons too. Today there is a great movement in the area of deliverance. We are beginning to realize that while in the womb and all the way to the tomb people are plagued by demonic spirits.

This book is an in-depth look at how we have power over demons, who can and should be delivered from them, and when they should be cast out. It teaches the deliverance minister what his or her attitude and physical being should be like. It teaches what should take place when working with children at different ages and even while they are in the womb. It alerts us to why we have some illnesses in our bodies as it is connected to unclean spirits, which are demons.

Thank God when we learn our authority and that the Word of God says we can cast demons out and then we can become free. We do have victory over the devil and his demons.

ACKNOWLEDGMENTS

$\mathcal{M}$Y GREATEST ACKNOWLEDGMENTS are to God the Father, God the Son, and God the Holy Spirit. The Holy Spirit has been my best teacher and is still my best teacher. He has taught me how to war in the realm of darkness. He has taught me how to discern evil spirits and cast them out of mankind. I thank God for giving me the mindset to compile a second book. (My first was *Beyond the Tears: Moving from Misery to Joy*, a biographical sketch about my life.)

I also want to acknowledge Margarette Ponds-Banks. She encouraged me to write this second book. She also was my consultant and researcher. So, I thank God for her.

I certainly am thankful to God for my five children who always encourage me with every endeavor I attempt. My daughter Kimberly Felisha (Dave) said, "Mom when are you going to start your next book?" Of course, that encouraged me to get out the pen and paper and start writing. Thanks, Kim. Of course, my eldest, Gary Lynn (Brenda), my oldest daughter, Vickie Rene (Terry), my next oldest son, Artez Dewayne (Dorinda), and my youngest son, Reginald Lamonte (LaShawn) all encourage me with writing, including their spouses, whom I love very much.

I want to acknowledge my editor, Dorinda Young, my son Artez's wife and the mother of two of my grandchildren.

My husband, Melvin Mayberry, whom I love very much, has been very encouraging and helpful, and I do so appreciate his love and support. He has tolerated my spending many long hours in writing and compiling this book.

"Elder Melvin Mayberry Sr. and Pastor Loreatha Gunnels Mayberry"

INTRODUCTION

WHETHER MANKIND REALIZES it or not, every day of our lives we are dealing with the spiritual realm as well as the natural or physical realm. The natural realm is the "run of the mill" of everyday life. When we are born, grow up through nurturing, and come into awareness (sitting alone, crawling, and then walking, learning to talk, etc.), we say it's "just life." It's not "just life." Many times it is also things we are dealing with in the spiritual realm of darkness where evil and unclean spirits reside. (It is a place where the devil is the father and leader.) Before he became the "prince of darkness," the devil was in charge of heaven's music until he wanted to become God and this was when he fell from heaven.

Satan, who is also called the devil, was not created with the character he became. These names mean adversary of God. He is also adversary of mankind.

Lucifer was the anointed cherub. Anointed means to be set apart for God's divine purpose. It also means "bestowal of God's divine favor" and "appointment to a special place or function." God had given [Lucifer, who became] Satan a certain amount of power and authority. But he perverted that power. Lucifer wanted to exalt himself above God rather than "just" being the Angel of God. Lucifer was created perfect in all his ways, but iniquity was found in him. It was *not* put there by God. Lucifer created it.[1]

He became full of pride. Ezekiel 28:17 states,

Thine heart was lifted up because of thy beauty, thou hast corrupted thy wisdom by reason of thy brightness: I will cast thee to the ground; I will lay thee before kings that they may behold thee.

Because the devil tried to raise himself above God, God kicked him out of the third heaven. Pride had set up in Lucifer's heart. Revelation 12:4–9 tells us when Lucifer was cast out of heaven by God, a third of all the angels were cast out with him. That's when he became Satan—the adversary of God and man. Second Corinthians 4:4 reads, "In whom the god of this world hath blinded the minds of them which believe not, lest the light of the glorious gospel of Christ, who is the image of God, should shine unto them."

Holy Spirit is the leader of the supernatural in the spiritual realm of light. There are angels that God sends out to protect us and keep us from stumbling (Luke

4:10–11). However, today we are focusing on unclean spirits and how they enter us and how to deal with them. The Bible tells us that there is spiritual warfare between the believers and the devil and his demons.

> Finally, my brethren, be strong in the Lord, and in the power of his might. Put on the whole armour of God, that ye may be able to stand against the wiles of the devil. For we wrestle not against flesh and blood, but against principalities, against powers, against the rulers of the darkness of this world, against spiritual wickedness in high places. Wherefore take unto you the whole armour of God, that ye may be able to withstand in the evil day, and having done all, to stand. Stand therefore, having your loins girt about with truth, and having on the breastplate of righteousness; And your feet shod with the preparation of the gospel of peace; Above all, taking the shield of faith, wherewith ye shall be able to quench all the fiery darts of the wicked. And take the helmet of salvation, and the sword of the Spirit, which is the word of God: Praying always with all prayer and supplication in the Spirit, and watching thereunto with all perseverance and supplication for all saints.
>
> —EPHESIANS 6:10–18

We do not know or understand all this before we are born again—that is, accept Jesus Christ as Lord. I might add, sometimes we do not know nor do we understand the reality of darkness. My knowledge was very limited before salvation and after salvation.

However, the Holy Spirit led me to Kenneth Hagin's book on deliverance, and He had me reading scriptures about how Jesus dealt with demons.

It was early in my Christian walk that I learned that deliverances will take place when the individual wants to be set free. However, sometimes when an individual gets close to an anointed person, they will manifest. If they are in an anointing service where the presence of God is very strong, they may manifest.

Don't forget that Jesus said we can do the same things He did when He walked the earth, and we can do even more because He is with the Father.

Very truly I tell you, whoever believes in me will do the works I have been doing, and they will do even greater things than these, because I am going to the Father. And I will do whatever you ask in my name, so that the Father may be glorified in the Son. You may ask me for anything in my name, and I will do it.

—JOHN 14:12–14, NIV

Chapter 1
BACKGROUND ON DEMONS

WHEN THE PROPHET in Grand Island, Nebraska, laid hands on me in 1999 during a local conference of churches and told me that God told him to release an apostolic mantle upon me during their presbyteries and prophetic team's ministry, God gave me authority to deal with the realm of darkness. Therefore, I am determined to walk in the footsteps of my Lord and Savior Jesus Christ who came to set the captives free.

> The Spirit of the Lord GOD is upon me; because the LORD hath anointed me to preach good tidings unto the meek; he hath sent me to bind up the brokenhearted, to proclaim liberty to the captives, and the opening of the prison to them that are bound.
>
> —ISAIAH 61:1

Yes, the Spirit of the Lord God came upon Jesus. When John the Baptist consented to baptize Him that prophecy would be fulfilled and He would be anointed to carry out the Father's call on His life (Matt. 3:16). That call and purpose was for Jesus to come and die that we would have eternal life. Jesus also performed miracles as He walked the earth for the three years He lived beyond His carpentry career.

My focus is on the brokenhearted, liberty to the captives, and the opening of prison doors. The brokenhearted are those who are deeply distressed and in trouble of any kind. There are many who are brokenhearted through broken relationships. Often we think that when we mention relationships it's all about husband and wife, girlfriend and boyfriend, or maybe platonic friendships. We also find relationships in our churches, on our jobs, in our families, and in our neighborhoods. Most often they are spiritual relationships.

A demon is an unclean spirit, a supernatural being, generally evil in nature that has the ability to affect humans through many different channels both internally and externally. Some demons need to be cast out and down.

Jesus was sent, not only to set the captives free but to open the prison for those who were bound. There are so many captives who need to be set free. Some may think the scripture in Isaiah is talking about people in a physical prison, mental institution, or nursing home; but please hear me. Some of those people are freer than those of us who are "free." So the scripture is speaking also of those who are spiritually bound and imprisoned. We can be spiritually bound in many ways. We can be bound with unforgiveness, rejection, sexual immorality, or addiction—just to name a few.

There is controversy about whether Christians have demons or not. Well the answer is yes. Christians can have demons. You will see next how they enter and where they enter. However, non-Christians not only can be carriers of demons in their souls, but they can also be possessed.

DEMONS CAN ENTER THE SOUL

We can be carriers of demons in our souls. You see, they cannot enter into our spirits because that's where God the Father, God the Holy Spirit, and God the Son dwell. But demons can enter our souls through:

- Eye gates

- Ear gates

- Tragedies and trauma

- Walking in unforgiveness

- Suffering rejections

- In the womb

- Deep hurt

Eye gates

Here is an example of how demons enter through the eye gates:

Bob and his mother wanted help from their pastor after Bob was set free. They were seeking advice on how he would remain free. They met at my house. I sat on my steps as the pastor, his wife, Bob, and his mother sat on my sofa and love seat. Bob began to tell the pastor and his wife what had happened the night of his deliverance. He told about how he walked home that night and imagined that he saw heads on fence posts and he began to run until he got home. It gives me chills to think back on that night while he was telling his story. He was seeing those horrific things because demons were already in his soul.

The reason it gives me chills is that as I watched him and listened to him, I could see the demon of fear. Because demons are spirits, I did not see a form but could see something like energy all over him. Needless to say, the demon of fear entered my eye gate. I was cold and could not sleep in my home, the home that I had come to love and loved being in alone after my youngest daughter married and moved away.

I began to sleep with the light on because I was so afraid. I would make sure I was home before dark and if I came in after dark, I was afraid to get out of my car and go into the house. It was not only in my soul, but it was upon me! I knew a fear demon was there, but I did not deal with it until later.

I was preparing to go to Mexico to minister and left Omaha about a week later. When I arrived in Mexico, I was bunking with six or seven women; but fear was so strong in and on me, I had to take something to help me fall asleep every night. An apostle was also on the trip to Mexico and I thought about asking him to deliver me from the spirit of fear but I didn't ask him, even though I knew he walked in deliverance.

When we returned to the United States, I called my granddaughter and asked her to come and stay with me for awhile because I feared staying alone. So she came and stayed with me for two weeks. I really don't know why I had not dealt with the spirit of fear! When I realized something in my past was bothering me, I went in my prayer room and dealt with rejection and forgave my parents. Because I was the youngest of ten children, I felt I had been left out of a lot of things. I began to fast and pray in my prayer room. Some days I would gag and spit; some days there would be nothing. After a week, my granddaughter asked me if it was okay if she left. I said "No, but I am getting there." That meant I was getting stronger and better but not yet delivered.

I kept going into my prayer room and saying, "In the name of Jesus Christ, I bind up the spirit of fear and cast you out of my soul." I pled the blood of Jesus. "You foul demon, you must leave. You do not have the right to be here because I am the daughter of the Most High God." I began to cough up foamy phlegm. A week later I told my granddaughter, "You can go home now; grandma is free."

Please note these two facts: (1) demons can enter into your eye gate, and (2) you can do deliverance on yourself. The foamy substance is not regurgitation material, but it is material from where the demons nested. One can have just eaten and not throw up the food that they just ate; instead it's the foamy "substance."

It is important to be careful what movies, television, and videos you watch. It is not good to watch movies showing a lot of flesh and lust, whether or not you are single or married, saved or unsaved; because through your eye gate, you could possibly receive the spirit of lust or of adultery if you watch a lot of sexual activity in the media mentioned. I believe actors can get into their parts so deep that their souls are wide open to a lot of demons, even to the point of being tormented to their death. Guard your eye gates and your soul.

Ear gates

It has been said that in some stores where soft music is playing there is a subliminal message that tells you to shop, shop, and shop until you drop. I don't know how true that is, but I do know that many times I go into stores and come out with things I never intended to buy or things I did not need because I already have the items at home.

A subliminal message is a message that is hidden or embedded or functioning below the threshold of consciousness. The word originates from Latin *sub*, meaning beneath, and *limen*, meaning threshold. These messages can come by way of recorded music, television, movies, and videotapes. The conscious mind is not aware of these messages, but they have an impact on the subconscious or deeper mind and on later behavior or attitudes. Sometimes subliminal messages are used in advertising and propaganda (brainwashing).

This brings me to the music of today that our young children are listening to by artists that sing about death and murder and sex and other evil things. I believe that is part of the reason some of our young people have no respect for life or death and do not have any hope. They kill each other like there is open season. They shoot each other. Young men and girls are both getting out of control. Some of the music artists say it is not their problem; that it is not their fault that the young people are out of control, killing each other and being sexually active at earlier and earlier ages. That is unbelievable. The shooters and killers are getting young and younger. Demons are taking over their lives, and they do not realize it until it is too late and they are behind prison doors and prison gates.

Tragedies and trauma

Tragedy can come so suddenly that a person's emotions are set up for oppression, depression, and even possession. It depends on how long the person waits to get help and whether or not they are walking in forgiveness and truth. If immediate help is received, then this will prevent things from manifesting in the soul.

My husband's first wife and the mother of his

children suddenly came down with breast cancer after they had been married for forty-two years. When she died, even though he had done all that was humanly possible to help and comfort her, he was tormented by the spirit of guilt and suicide. I discerned all these spirits while we were talking on the phone one day; and I said, "I bind up the spirit of torment, the spirit of guilt, and the spirit of suicide and cast you out in the name of Jesus Christ." He began to cough and he coughed for a little while. And then I prayed for him. You should always pray and release an anointing upon the delivered person.

One night we had visitors come in our church. A prophecy was going to be given to the visitors when they came. There was a gentleman there who had lost his wife to death, and it had been two years since she had passed. My pastor and some other leaders went over to pray for him. I decided to go over and just lay hands on him for him to receive peace.

As I stood over him, I could smell the presence of demons that he carried. We will call him Bill. After we were dismissed and Bill was standing, someone said that he had just lost his wife two years ago. God showed me he had not grieved the passing of his wife. So I asked Bill, "Have you grieved the passing of your wife?" He said that he had not. God showed me he was being tormented with guilt, and I told him that. One of the church elders said to me, "There you go. Go deliver him." I went towards him and he began to manifest. His face began to change from its normal form. One of the church members and the elder who had told me, "There you go," came along side me to help pray; and I completed the deliverance. He was set free of guilt. Bill left a free man!

As I watched television about a murder-suicide incident where a young man entered a local department store and shot and wounded people, I realized that explained the heavy police presence that we encountered as we had headed west on Interstate 80. There were so many police cars that came barreling past us that I could not count them. They exited at the North Freeway. This young man, not only wounded and killed other people, he turned the weapon on himself and committed suicide. According to the news media this young man's mental issues began at about the age of four.

A few years ago, God revealed to me that babies are born into the world innocent and there are things which may happen along the way that cause them to turn out a certain way. It may not be in the womb or the delivery room that they are invaded by evil spirits. Although mental illness is not always due to evil spirits, I believe that to be the case here. Many times the parents divorce, as was the case with this young man. When parents divorce, often the child thinks, "What did I do? If I had been a better child, my parents would still be together."

Then the child begins to act out by rebelling and showing a lot of anger. This can set the child up for hatred, bitterness, and unforgiveness. Then it is possible the child will develop low self-esteem with a feeling of worthlessness. I contend that a spirit of evil feels like it has a right to move into the soul or even possess the individual in some cases, possibly in this case. I believe this particular child went through so much that the spirit of death entered and convinced him he needed to end it all and that it was a great idea to go out "in style" by taking others with him. I believe, further, he felt no one cared and would be glad if he was no longer on the earth.

I think there are young people by the hundreds, similar to this young man, who have no hope. They are a part of gangs as their families. Death means nothing to them; or maybe I should say life means nothing to them. My understanding is that young Black males are fathering a large number of children for the purpose of continuing their legacy because they don't have high expectations of longevity.

I sense God the Father soon will walk the streets of Omaha, Nebraska, and the stronghold over that area will be forced to set free every young, middle-aged, and older person from crack cocaine, alcohol, "ice," and any other drug and prostitution, murder, and the gay lifestyle. I further believe the crack houses and bars will close down. The gang members and other sinners will run to the altars and ask, "What do I need to do to be saved?" (Acts 16:30). The Omaha newspaper will state, "Surely God has visited Omaha."

When I was part of an intercessory group approximately ten years ago, a prophetic word came forth that the strongman (the controlling spirit) in Omaha is pride, a throne of pride. And I believe it has never been destroyed because rebellion is a twin to witchcraft and a sister to pride. We are not fighting against flesh and blood but evil spirits in high places (Eph. 6:12).

Walking in unforgiveness

When we do not forgive, it opens the door to the enemy (devil) to send in demons to set up in our souls. They may manifest in

- Hatred

- Bitterness

- Arthritis

- High blood pressure

- Ulcers

You are suffering. But the person you are holding unforgiveness for has gone on about his or her business—gone on vacation and is having a great time on a beach somewhere—while you are a carrier of an unforgiving spirit and need deliverance.

Suffering rejections

Often times when growing up we suffer some kind of rejection. Perhaps you grew up in a large family and there were favorites of your parents', or among your siblings you never got any hugs. You began to think you are the "black sheep" of the family. You feel unloved, unwanted.

Typically, parents don't know how to express their love to their children. My mother always told us, "I love all my children." But I never had her tell me, "I love you Loreatha," (Rea). I am pretty sure she never received a lot of hugs (if any) because her mother died when she was five years old and she was raised by a single dad—my grandfather who had been a slave. When I would visit Morrilton, Arkansas, and it was time for me to leave my mother's house, I was always the one who had to reach out to kiss her goodbye. There was no response.

After I gave my life to Christ, I learned what it was to reach out to my children with love. I tell them how much I love them. I also hug them and my grandchildren because I love them. I have been a role model for them. They love their children and are able to tell them they love them. I had to learn through the Holy Spirit, for He is my best teacher.

If you talk to many children of today, you will find many of them carriers of bitterness and rebellion. And it is because the parents never hugged them or told them, "I love you." Oh, they saw to it the children had clothes and oftentimes an education; but they never gave them the time of day. Again, if you check their background, you will find they never received hugs nor were they told they were loved. I have broken the curse of rejection in that area.

I have a friend that when I started to give her hugs and tell her I loved her, it was very, very awkward for her. Now that she is in a church and working for the kingdom of God, it is much easier for her. She was drawing back because she was the oldest child and was always told what to do around the house and what to do for her siblings but she was never hugged or told that she was loved and appreciated. So, I witnessed bitterness and rebellion towards her parents. She received deliverance from me at sixty-two years of age. She forgave her parents.

Additional areas of rejection:

- Perhaps you are or were in an unhealthy marriage where the husband did not pay you the attention you needed or deserved.

- Perhaps one of you became an adulterer or just gave all others compliments except you.

- Perhaps he or she stayed away from home all hours of the night.

- Perhaps he or she bought things for his or her self and the children but never anything for you.

- Perhaps you were not chosen in your church to preach yet you were ordained in that same church.

- Perhaps the first man or woman you believed God brought into your life to be your soul mate was not the person you thought he or she to be.

- Perhaps rejection began in childhood or during adulthood.

- Perhaps rejection can be something minor or it can be so devastating that you just cannot get past it.

- Perhaps rejection gives a sense of not being cared about or not being wanted.

- Perhaps rejection can begin in the womb.

For the woman God still offers these words of comfort:

> Fear not; for thou shalt not be ashamed: neither be thou confounded; for thou shalt not be put to shame: for thou shalt forget the shame of thy youth, and shalt not remember the reproach of thy widowhood any more. For thy Maker is thine husband; the LORD of hosts is his name; and thy Redeemer the Holy One of Israel; The God of the whole earth shall he be called. For the LORD hath called thee as a woman forsaken

and grieved in spirit, and a wife of youth, when thou wast refused, saith thy God.

—ISAIAH 54:4–6

This illustration shows how a wife can be deserted and distressed in spirit—a wife who married young, only to be rejected. But as I mentioned earlier, sometimes it can be the man receiving rejection from his wife.

You also can feel ashamed and betrayed if the rejection comes from your siblings. My own siblings are a lot older than I am. There are only four of us living now, but I remember "back in the day" when they were all alive and in the prime of life, I felt strong rejection. Before I continue, I might add they did not set out to be cruel to me—at least I don't believe that to be so. However, if I tried to join their conversation I was made to feel dumb as a box of rocks. Some slight remarks would be made about my statement and I would go sliding off like a dog dragging his tail.

I grew past rejection; but there are millions of people who are still suffering from the root of rejection. Hebrews 12:15 says, "Looking diligently lest any man fail of the grace of God; lest any root of bitterness springing up trouble you, and thereby many be defiled." Remember Bob who received deliverance and how strong bitterness had set up in his soul? Well, he had a root of bitterness.

Here is another example of how rejection can set up

in the soul at a very early age. The story comes from Derek Prince in *God's Remedy for Rejection*:

> Many years ago I was conducting services at a church in Miami. While visiting one of the parishioners at home a few nights earlier, I had done something I rarely do. I said to her, "Sister, if I'm correct, you have the spirit of death in you." She had every reason to be happy, but she never was. She had a good husband and children, yet she hardly ever smiled or looked happy. She was like a person in continual mourning. Although I very rarely make that kind of statement to anybody, I felt I had to say something to her that night. I said, "I am preaching on Friday night in Miami. If you come, I will pray for you." At the beginning of the meeting, I noticed her sitting in the front row. Once again, I did something I do not usually do. At a certain point in the service, I walked over to her and said, "You spirit of death, in the name of Jesus, I command you to answer me now. When did you enter this woman?" And the spirit, not the woman, answered very clearly, "When she was two years old." I said, "How did you get in?" Again it was the spirit that answered, "Oh, she felt rejected; she felt unwanted; she felt lonely." Later that evening the woman was delivered from the spirit of death.[1]

I have named some instances of rejection, but I am going to continue with "hard core rejection" where spirits have set up in the soul and need casting out by one who has authority in the spiritual realm. This rejection includes:

- Divorce

- Poverty

- Child abuse

- Abandonment

- Parental neglect

- Public humiliation

- Unwanted pregnancy

- Failure at work

- Failure at school

All of the above instances can bring rejection and become deep-seated in the soul.

When counseling with a seventeen-year-old young woman, I discovered she felt strong rejection from her father, sister, and a brother. She believed they did not care about her or love her. And to my surprise, she felt like her grandmother had also stopped loving her because she said the grandmother did not spend time with her as she had in the past. I assured her that the father and the siblings loved her, but I asked her if it could be that they had issues of their own. As we continued to talk, I had an impression that the grandmother was not intentionally rejecting her but simply had an extremely busy lifestyle.

Rejection in the womb or at birth

If rejection takes place in the womb, infancy, or in childhood, it brings with it feelings of betrayal and shame. It may cause low self-esteem and shame or the person may not develop trust. There are millions of women and men out there who have been damaged in this manner. I will share some other points on rejection in the womb or at birth:

- Women who have an unexpected pregnancy may become upset and call it a mistake.

- Women who never wanted children and are completely outraged at the very thought of being pregnant may discuss abortion freely with their friends and family and/or their mate.

- The husband or a boyfriend who does not want the baby may suggest abortion.

- The trauma of childbirth may allow demons to enter a baby. My mother said death passes over a woman seven times while she is in labor. (It is my opinion that the delivery room can be a dangerous place.)

• Sometimes while the child is still in the womb, demons may enter the baby or will try to kill it.

Let me provide you with an example: My oldest daughter gave birth to a daughter. The pregnancy seemed to be progressing well, when all of a sudden the doctor seemed "out of sorts," with a frown on his face. The nurses were running around like chickens with their heads cut off. It did not take a rocket scientist to see that something had gone wrong.

My great-niece was present during the delivery. My youngest daughter and I began to pray in tongues (an unknown language) and my great-niece prayed with her mind. As quickly as things had turned for the worst, they returned to normal. We had gone into the spiritual realm of darkness and dealt with that murderous spirit or spirits. My oldest daughter shared later that the nurse wanted to break her water to advance the labor. But she did not agree to it because her doctor had not arrived at the hospital. After the birth of her baby, the doctor told her if she had allowed the nurse to break her water the baby would have choked to death. He told her the umbilical cord had a knot in it as large as an orange and was wrapped around its neck.

My youngest daughter who had a baby boy experienced no problems.

Deep hurt

Deep hurt is immeasurable. What might hurt one person deeply may not affect the next person in the same manner. I believe that deep hurt can be so deep that the person receiving deep wounds enters into unforgiveness, hatred, and bitterness and is brought to the place whereby he or she needs deliverance, especially if it is not dealt with in a timely manner.

I was deeply hurt over a relationship that ended and I had to hand over to my partner the house we purchased together. In my first book, titled *Beyond the Tears: Moving from Misery to Joy*, I spoke in depth about that relationship and how the deep hurt caused unforgiveness to set up in my soul.

I would like to note that men and women have committed suicide because they are so deeply hurt because a wife, husband, or boyfriend ends their relationship. They will end their life because the devil tells them they cannot live without that person. Of course, the devil is the father of all lies according to John 8:44. Consequently they were open to the spirit of hurt and rejection, and of course, suicide to set up in their souls.

Many times when a couple has been together for forty, fifty, or sixty years and one passes away, the other one is so deeply hurt that the spirit of death sets up in the soul and the person soon passes away. We say they grieved themselves to death. It is my opinion they had help of the spirit of death and also the spirit of depression and loneliness. The bad thing about it is they do not want any help; they want to die, not realizing they need deliverance, which would bring hope to him or her again.

A young man we will call Joe (who is not a young man any more) was so deeply in love with his wife that when she passed away he became an alcoholic. Before her death he was a social drinker. I still see him wandering down the street aimlessly as though he has nothing left to live for. He was hurt so deeply by his wife's death that he gave up on life and became an addict. I believe that because of the deep hurt and the addiction he has become possessed and needs help though deliverance. I know and I understand everything is not caused by demons. Some alcoholics can overcome the addiction through strong resistance of the drug or by becoming a Christian.

We do not realize the harm that is done to us and our lives by not dealing with things when they come up. Beelzebub is always there to slip through whatever crack that is left open or unprotected. His ultimate goal is to control or inhabit you if he can, then you will become a slave to sin. He can and will possess you if you are straddling the fence. To be clearer, you go to church, you praise and worship God, and then you leave to go and willfully sin. Do not hide deep hurt. If you do not have someone to trust, vent to a stranger who you pray you will never see again. Ask God to help you forgive them for their actions or their verbal insults. That will shut the enemy down every time.

To further establish that demons do enter the soul or can enter the spirit, soul, and body, we will use the following scriptures:

In Mark 5:1–15 we see that demons that can possess a man may also enter animals. There was a mad man of Gadara who was possessed with the devil and had an army of demon spirits inside him. When Jesus delivered the demoniac, the evil spirits didn't want Him to send them out of the country, so they asked Jesus to send them into a herd of swine. Jesus gave them permission to enter the swine.

The Word of God also tells us in that same scripture that the man lived in a tomb and had a legion of demons that caused him to tear off his clothes, wander around naked, and cut himself with stones. His actions were a manifestation of the unclean spirits that possessed him. When an unclean spirit controls a person or embodies him or her, it makes the person unclean.

Matthew records another incident in chapter 17:

> And when they were come to the multitude, there came to him a certain man, kneeling down to him, and saying, Lord, have mercy on my son: for he is a lunatic, and sore vexed: for oftentimes he falleth into the fire, and oft into the water. And I brought him to thy disciples, and they could not cure him. Then Jesus answered and said, O faithless and perverse generation, how long shall I be with you? how long shall I suffer you? bring him hither to me. And Jesus rebuked the devil; and he departed out of him: and the

child was cured from that very hour. Then came the disciples to Jesus apart, and said, Why could not we cast him out? and Jesus said unto them, Because of your unbelief: for verily I say unto you, If ye have faith as a grain of mustard seed, ye shall say unto this mountain, Remove hence to yonder place; and it shall remove; and nothing shall be impossible unto you.

—MATTHEW 17:14–20

Evidently the young man had some kind of seizures similar to epilepsy and couldn't talk because of it. We see in this scripture that the disciples were not able to cast the demon out. In Mark 9:29, the Bible states that some demons only come out through fasting and praying. We have to believe that we have the authority to cast out demons.

When the emotional area of our souls has been attacked, we are in a place that feels like there is neither hope nor a chance for healing. It has been said that no matter what it is, time will heal all things. I contend that is a myth; time does not heal everything. Whatever the hurt may be, one can come to a place of toleration but not to a place of complete healing. There are some ways to get set free from deep hurt. Dr. Basil Frasure's article, "The Wounded Heart," shines light on how to overcome deep hurt and not just toleration.

When you have deep hurt, you need the hand of God to move so you can and will be set free. This is expressed well in Psalm 109:22: "For I am afflicted and needy, and my heart is wounded within me" (NAS). Dr.

Frasure gives us the definition of a wounded heart as follows: "A wounded heart occurs when someone or something brings hurt to your emotions."[2] This concept is affirmed in both Proverbs 18:8 and 26:22: "The words of a talebearer are as wounds, and they go down into the innermost of the belly."

Dr. Frasure gives the following sources of hurts:

1. Result of offenses brought to us from others. (People say and do things to hurt us.) Proverbs 18:8.

2. Result from own sinful behavior. Psalm 25:18; Proverbs 17:19; 2 Samuel 24:10.

3. Result from calamity where one is overcome by the experience. Job 3:23–26.

4. Result of the sins of the forefathers. Exodus 34:6–7.

5. Result from drug and alcohol use. Proverbs 23:29–35

6. Result from occult involvement. Leviticus 20:6.[3]

People can and will say things to hurt us. In other words, people will talk about you, and it does not have to be something they know but information that has been passed around like an old pair of shoes. Each time it is told, it gets further away from the truth.

Someone will always make sure you hear what is being said about you because they want you to know—not to help you, but to hurt and wound you. Many times you will find your "so-called" friends are at the root of the gossip. Depending on what is being spread all over the place, you, me, or the individual who is at the brunt of it all may become ashamed and depressed.

Our own sins can bring us deep hurt. This is well expressed in Psalm 25:18: "Look upon my afflictions and my pain; and forgive all my sins." For examples of how our sins can bring us deep hurt, God tells us not to be unequally yoked (2 Cor. 6:14). He is telling us not to marry one who is not a believer. When we do marry someone who is not a believer, there are repercussions. Perhaps one is adulterous and the other is not and believes in the principles of God. This type of action could bring deep hurt. Proverbs 17:19 has a different slant on the effects caused by our own sin: "He who loves a quarrel loves sin; he who builds a high gate invites destruction" (NIV). Second Samuel 24:10, "David's heart smote him" after he sinned, depicts how we can bring deep hurt upon ourselves through our own sin. Job was overwhelmed by the tragedies that befell him (Job 3:25–26), illustrating that through a calamity, the heart can be wounded.

The Bible helps us understand that what our forefathers have done can affect us and cause us deep hurt (Exod. 34:7). Everyone has to pay for their own sin. However, if your father was an adulterer, then it is possible that you could walk that same path through generational curses. Therefore, deep hurt would come to the person who was cheated on when it is discovered. The Bible also states that everything that goes on in the dark shall come to the light (1 Cor. 4:5).

The results of drug and alcohol use can bring very deep hurt to the person and to others. Motor vehicle homicide can be caused while a person is driving under the influence of drugs or alcohol. This causes deep hurt to all those involved.

> Who hath woe? who hath sorrow? who hath contentions? who hath babbling? who hath wounds without cause? who hath redness of eyes? They that tarry long at the wine; they that go to seek mixed wine. Look not thou upon the wine when it is red, when it giveth his colour in the cup, when it moveth itself aright. At the last it biteth like a serpent, and stingeth like an adder. Thine eyes shall behold strange women, and thine heart shall utter perverse things. Yea, thou shalt be as he that lieth down in the midst of the sea, or as he that lieth upon the top of a mast. They have stricken me, shalt thou say, and I was not sick; they have beaten me, and I felt it not: when shall I awake? I will seek it yet again.
>
> —PROVERBS 23:29–35

Involvement in the occult, it tells us in Leviticus 20:6, results in the person being cut off from their people. This occurs repeatedly and the families are wounded deeply—wounded because it is as though they have lost the family member to death.

According to Dr. Frasure, "Hurts *never* just goes away! Time will not bring complete healing to them. Whenever you remember the experience, you *feel* the hurt. Some people will even block out their memory so they won't have to face *feeling* the hurts, but they are still there."[4] Dr. Frasure shares a few symptoms of deep hurt:

1. Physical—Proverbs 17:22
   Nerve Disorders
   Allergies
   Stomach problems
   Heart aches [heart problems]
   Insomnia

2. Mental—Proverbs 18:14
   Depression
   Fits of anger and rage
   Confusion
   Various fears
   Shyness
   Dominance

3. Spiritual—Matthew 18:34
   Nightmares
   Hearing voices
   Seeing unusual things
   Lack of control of self[5]

According to Dr. Frasure, "Some people respond by backing away from the situation to allow time for healing. They often turn inward and brood over their hurts. The hurts become like a *big sore risen* just waiting for someone to prick it with a sharp word, *then* out comes all of the corruption of *anger, bitterness, hate, revenge, and fear.* The rejection they then receive brings more hurts."[6]

All that is very true! For over a year I did deliverance for a local church. One of the young women who I worked with had suppressed a molestation that had taken place when she was four years old. Something happened that caused her to remember the perversion. The hurt and shame was buried deeply and was affecting her marriage—for about thirty-five years she had locked the hurt away in her heart.

Dr. Frasure's instructions for inner healing include:

1. Forgive the person who has offended you
   (Matthew 6:12, 14–15; 18:21–35).
   Others
   God
   Self

2. Place the judgment of the offender/s into
   God's hands and ask Him to forgive
   them (Luke 23:34; Acts 7:6).

3. Confess your own sins to God: unforgiveness, anger, bitterness, hate, revenge,
thoughts of murder, suicide, guilt, fear, etc.

   a. Ask God to forgive you and cleanse
   you (1 John 1:9). A wound needs to
   be cleansed of dirt before it can be
   healed.

   b. If you feel that anger or something
   else is still there, then [pursue deliv-
   erance]: (A wound needs to be
   cleansed of infection also).[7]

I say when inner healing takes place then "hands on"
deliverance will not have to take place by a deliverance
minister. The main thing I want to point out is that we
can be set free. We will discover later how to remain free.

OTHER DEMONIC ENTRYWAYS

Outside the individual

Demons can oppress from outside the individual.
Being oppressed by a demon is not the same as being
possessed from the spirit, soul, and body. When the
spirit, soul, and body are taken over, the person is possessed of a demon or demons like the mad man of
Gadara. But to be oppressed is from outside the body;
it is not an embodiment itself. When a demon does
find embodiment in a person, it tends to make that
person become what it is.

We contend that when we see people who think that

29

they are female and they were born male or the person thinks she is male when she was born female, what's really happening here is that a demon of homosexuality has entered the spirit, soul, and body of that individual causing the individual to desire and act like the opposite sex. I do not believe that people are born homosexual. But they may have a generational curse because Scripture tells us that this is unnatural:

> Wherefore God also gave them up to uncleanness through the lusts of their own hearts, to dishonor their own bodies between themselves: Who changed the truth of God into a lie, and worshipped and served the creature more than the Creator, who is blessed for ever. Amen. For this cause God gave them up unto vile affections: for even their women did change the natural use into that which is against nature: And likewise also the men, leaving the natural use of the woman, burned in their lust one toward another; men with men working that which is unseemly, and receiving in themselves that recompense of their error which was meet. And even as they did not like to retain God in their knowledge, God gave them over to a reprobate mind, to do those things which are not convenient.
>
> —ROMANS 1:24–28

A revelation:

While I was writing about the spirit of rejection entering the baby in the womb, a revelation came to me that a homosexual spirit could also enter the baby while it is in the womb. Therefore, he or she would be born a carrier of that spirit.

The physical body

Demons can also enter the flesh of the body, the joints, etc. They will and can oppress, depress, and possess the individual *without* entering into the soul. Not all physical afflictions are caused by demonic activity or demons. Sometimes, however, demons seek to possess mankind because they need a body in order to find their fullest expression in this physical world. They are spirits so they need a body to operate and to have greater freedom to manifest in the natural realm. They could manifest in the soul and body of an individual, causing him or her to desire and act like the opposite sex.

Of course, they can manifest to a degree in the spiritual realm even without a body. They can make themselves heard, felt, and known. They come to oppress the person.

Generational curse

Many sicknesses are spiritual and many are passed down through the bloodlines called iniquity, better known as a generational curse.

> Finally, my brethren be strong in the Lord, and in the power of his might. Put on the whole armour of God, that ye may be able to stand against the wiles of the devil. For we wrestle not against flesh and blood, but against principalities,

against powers, against the rulers of the darkness of this world, against spiritual wickedness in high places.

—Ephesians 6:10–12

Since we are not fighting against flesh and blood, we must understand where a lot of our bondage and depression comes from. Of course, a door has to be open, in one sense, for demons to operate in our lives. However, he may come in as a thief in the night (John 10:10). We do not have to allow the devil and his demons to come into our lives and control us; whether it is through the door of generational curses, the very words of our lips, what we listen to, or what we watch. When we identify a generational curse, we need to go in and break it off of our lives and our children's and grandchildren's lives.

An example of a curse would be the fact that I got pregnant at fourteen years of age and my daughters got pregnant out of wedlock at young ages. Many times a mother can have breast cancer and their daughters will have breast cancer. Iniquity means to be bent in a particular direction or thing; so, if a father or mother has a drinking problem, most likely the children will already be bent in that direction and they will become alcoholics. An example of this would be that my oldest son's father's family moved in (or with) the alcoholic demon, so when he grew older he began to drink a lot. I might add that the child does not have to be around the parents to move in the habit of addiction, if that's the curse. The curse could be adultery, and they would

commit adultery unless the curse was broken. We
need to become educated on generational curses so we
can walk in the authority given to us by God.

> Behold, I give unto you power to tread on ser-
> pents and scorpions, and over all the power of
> the enemy: and nothing shall by any means hurt
> you.
>
> —LUKE 10:19

The word *power* in this scripture in the Greek language means authority over the devil and his demons.
He says *all* of the power, not *some* of the power.

> Ye are of God, little children, and have overcome
> them: because greater is he that is in you, than
> he that is in the world.
>
> —1 JOHN 4:4

We need to be careful of our actions and words. That
is, do not leave a door open to the devil. As a matter-
of-fact, he only needs a crack to slip in and do damage
in your life or my life. We are talking about getting
set free of demons and *staying* free. You will see later
how we stay free. Right now let's continue to look at
things that allow demons to get into our souls and our
becoming carriers of them. They come and cause sickness and disease to set up in our bodies—diseases like
diabetes, cancer, high blood pressure, etc.

The open door of our mouths

Demons can enter through the words of our mouth. Let us look at the words of our mouth; we can have what we speak. Our words are powerful.

> Death and life are in the power of the tongue: and they that love it shall eat the fruit there of.
>
> —PROVERBS 18:21

We will say, "My mother or my father had diabetes, so I know I cannot get around it and sometime down the road I will have it. I might as well get ready for it." Or, "Cancer runs in my family, and it is at a certain age that I can expect cancer to manifest." And guess what? It will—by the fruit of your mouth. Or you say, "I get sick this time every year with sinus problems and colds." Expect it. Begin to stock up on over-the-counter medication to be ready for the illness!

Transference

Because demons are transferable:

1. Do not do deliverance with little children in the room.

2. Do not do deliverance with a team member if they are unclean (in sin) because the spirit is looking for a body. Therefore, if the minister casts it out of the person receiving ministry, it is possible for it to enter the unclean team member.

When I ministered deliverance to the gentleman with the spirit of guilt and torment, the spirit (demon) entered one of the women who were praying with me to set him free. The team member started coughing really hard and had to stop praying because the demon of guilt had entered her. She had committed sin and was feeling guilty about it. She had repented to God for the sin but, again, the guilt was still there. The pastor who was present at the time was able to calm her down. He stated that demons cannot jump from one person to another, but they can.

Approximately a year before this experience, I had another situation where I was working with a young man in whom I discerned the spirit of bitterness. As I cast it out of him, it entered his aunt who was sitting on the foot of the bed interceding while I prayed. I looked around at her and asked, "Did you see that?" I said that because it was very foul and evil and I thought it had gone out of the window. But then I realized it had entered the aunt. The look on her face was indescribable. She looked as though she was part of a horror movie. Her head was moving swiftly and looking around the room. Then I knew it had entered her, and I cast it out.

TYPES OF DEMONS

I believe that individuals are imprisoned when they are held captive by a demon or demons. We contend they are held prisoners within their own bodies. I am not speaking of possession, however. If one does not get help, the demon can set up possession and the individual will begin to act out the kind of demon that entered the person.

Let's read where Peter preached to Cornelius and his household:

> That word, I say, ye know, which was published throughout all Judea, and began from Galilee, after the baptism which John preached; How God anointed Jesus of Nazareth with the Holy Ghost and with power: who went about doing good, and healing all that were oppressed of the devil; for God was with him.
>
> —ACTS 10:37–38

Peter is calling sickness and disease satanic oppression.

The following are some of the types of demons that look for entryways. I will look at more precise types of demons and their action in future chapters.

Lying spirit

A lying spirit causes a person to lie. All liars will go to hell unless there is repentance and forgiveness (Rev. 21:8).

Blind spirit

The Word of God tells us that when Jesus was dealing with a blind person, He was dealing with a blind spirit.

Then was brought unto him one possessed with
a devil, blind, and dumb: and he healed him,
insomuch that the blind and dumb both spake
and saw.

—MATTHEW 12:22

Deaf spirit

The Word of God also speaks of a deaf spirit. This
may mean the spirit is present and must be dealt with
before the person can hear.

When Jesus saw that the people came running
together, he rebuked the foul spirit, saying unto
him, Thou dumb and deaf spirit, I charge thee,
come out of him, and enter no more into him.

—MARK 9:25

Let's look at what happened when Jesus came down
from the Mount of Transfiguration. Jesus stated in
John 14:12:

Verily, verily I say unto you, he that believeth
on me, the works that I do shall he do also; and
greater works than these shall he do; because I
go unto my Father.

Jesus let us know He was ascending to heaven to sit
on the right hand of God and He was leaving authority
and power in our hands. He says in John 14:14: "If ye
shall ask anything in my name, I will do it." And in
Mark 16:17: "And these signs shall follow them that
believe; in my name shall they cast out devils."

As a new Christian in the late 1980s, after falling a

few times, I just about "ate" the Word of God (Bible). I read night and day. I not only read the Bible but I read the material that the Bible supported. A lot of that material was written by Kenneth E. Hagin, whom God healed of heart trouble at age seventeen. One of the subjects was about dealing with demons from the book *Demons and How to Deal with Them.*[8]

I never thought God would call me to be a deliverance minister. However, He did. I never sought it on my own. One reason for that was because I had read the scripture that told about imitators of Paul who were beaten by an evil spirit at Ephesus. They were beaten out of their clothes. That scripture reads as follows:

> Then certain of the vagabond Jews, exorcists, took upon them to call over them which had evil spirits the name of the Lord Jesus, saying, We adjure by Jesus whom Paul preacheth. And there were seven sons of one Sceva, a Jew, and the chief of the priests, which did so. And the evil spirit answered and said, Jesus I know, and Paul I know, but who are ye? And the man in whom the evil spirit was leaped on them, and overcame them, and prevailed against them, so that they fled out of that house naked and wounded.
>
> —Acts 19:13–16

We will see later on why this would happen to a person attempting deliverance when we talk about being prepared to do deliverance in chapter 4, "The Deliverance Minister."

And he said unto them, Go ye into all the world, and preach the gospel to every creature. He that believeth and is baptized shall be saved; but he that believeth not shall be damned. And these signs shall follow them that believe; In my name shall they cast out devils; they shall speak with new tongues; They shall take up serpents; and if they drink any deadly thing, it shall not hurt them; they shall lay hands on the sick, and they shall recover.

—MARK 16:15–18

USING SPIRITUAL GIFTS TO RECOGNIZE DEMONS

Now concerning spiritual gifts, brethren, I would have you not ignorant. Ye know that ye were Gentiles, carried away unto these dumb idols, even as ye were led. Wherefore I give you to understand, that no man speaking by the Spirit of God, calleth Jesus accursed: and that no man can say that Jesus is the Lord, but by the Holy Ghost. Now there are diversities of gifts, but the same Spirit. And there are differences of administrations, but the same Lord. And there are diversities of operations, but it is the same God which worketh all in all. But the manifestation of the Spirit is given to every man to profit withal. For the one is given by the Spirit the word of wisdom; to another the word of knowledge by the same Spirit; To another, faith by the same Spirit; to another the gift of healing by the same Spirit; To another the working of miracles; to another prophecy; to

another discerning of spirits; to another divers
kinds of tongues; to another the interpretation
of tongues; But all these worketh that one and
the selfsame Spirit, dividing to every man sev-
erally as he will. For as the body is one, and
hath many members, and all the members of
that one body, being many, are one body: so
also is Christ. For by One Spirit we are all baptized into one body, whether we be Jews or
Gentiles, whether we be bond or free; and have
been all made to drink into one Spirit. For the
body is not one member, but many.

—1 CORINTHIANS 12:1–14

As you can see in the above scripture, God has given
us spiritual gifts to profit all mankind. They are of the
same Spirit (Holy Spirit); however, they all operate dif-
ferently for recognizing demons. I will concentrate
only on three of the nine gifts, which are gifts of revelation. We will look at all three gifts; however, I will
expound on how gift of discerning of spirits during
deliverance is of primary importance because this gift
allows you to see into the spiritual realm to know with
which demon you are dealing.

I will share with you how each gift operates, beginning with the gift of the word of wisdom:

Gift of the word of wisdom

The gift of the word of wisdom reveals the future
through the manifestation of the Holy Spirit. "The
Word of Wisdom is a supernatural revelation by the
Spirit of God concerning the Divine purpose and plan

in the mind and will of God. The word 'wisdom' is the best gift because it is a revelation concerning the plans and purposes in the mind of God."[9]

The office of the prophet usually operates with this manifestation. The deliverance minister, if he or she operates out of the office of the prophet, may begin to express things, not only of the past and present but also the future. During the interview or during a spiritual service, the minister may state, "You have been suffering from loneliness that has brought depression. But stop worrying because in six months God is going to bring you a husband, and he is wealthy and he is a pastor." In this statement the past, present, and future was dealt with. Through that revelation it would be known that a spirit of loneliness and depression was oppressing the person. Then those spirits can be dealt with by casting them out or down.

With this example you have witnessed the operation of both the word of knowledge and the word of wisdom. Some people think that Solomon's wisdom was a gift of the word of wisdom but it was not. His wisdom was given to him by God. It was the kind of wisdom written of in the Book of James 1:5: "If any of you lack wisdom, let him ask of God, that giveth to all men liberally, and upbraideth not; and it shall be given him."

When Solomon became king he cried out to God to give him wisdom to deal with the large number of people he was to lead (2 Chron. 1:10). God told him

He would give him wisdom, plus bless him to be rich because he only asked for wisdom. There is an account in 1 Kings 3:16–28 where two women each had a baby. One of the babies died. Both women claimed the baby who was left alive. Solomon told them he would cut the baby in half and give each woman a half. That caused the real mother to cry out, "Give the baby to her!" Solomon used wisdom, but it was not the gift of the word of wisdom.

God has promised to give every man or woman what I call "common wisdom" that is given to everyone who asked for it. The gift of the word of wisdom is *not* given to everyone, only to those whom God chooses to give it.

Gift of the word of knowledge

"The Word of Knowledge is a supernatural revelation by the Spirit of God concerning certain facts in the mind of God."[10] The Spirit of God manifests through people who have received these gifts. The Holy Spirit manifests with the word of knowledge to be given to another to profit that person and is of the past and present. Perhaps during the interview God may reveal that the person was raped or molested at an early age. It could be that God would only show you the molestation and not the perpetrator because He reveals in part. As I work with the person, if there is more, God may reveal or expose more reasons for deliverance.

"The difference between the two gifts—the Word of Knowledge and the Word of Wisdom—is that the revelation the Word of Knowledge is always present tense or concerning something has happened in the past. On the other hand, the Word of Wisdom always speaks of the future."[11]

Gift of the discerning of spirits

In 1 Corinthians 12:10 we learned that there is a gift of discerning of spirits. The word *discerning* in the Greek is the word *dandiakrisis*, which means judging through, seeing through. This gift has been defined as "the supernatural ability given by the Holy Spirit to perceive the source of a spiritual manifestation and determine whether it is of God (Acts 10:30–35), of the devil (Acts 16:16–18), of man (Acts 8:18–23), or of the world."[12]

There are three sources of spirits:

- Human

- Satanic—meaning demonic

- God—divine, angelic spirits

Also, there are three levels of discerning:

- Natural—comes from knowing how to "read" people

- Psychic—meaning in the mind; (soul power) the truth of the matter is that man has tremendous mind abilities.

There is a lot of power in our brains that
is given by Satan.

- Divine Gifts—the supernatural ability to
  see into three realms of the spirit:
    The kingdom of darkness—demons
    The kingdom of light—angelic
    The Holy Spirit—the Spirit of Truth

Note that all supernatural activity is not of God. If it
is the Spirit of God, usually it will give witness in your
spirit. This gift is used to discern evil spirits and their
devices or names. Many times discerning of spirits is
confused with understanding human behavior (people
just knowing people).

The three gifts are greatly manifested during the
deliverance itself but that is not the only time the gifts
manifest. They also manifest during the interview and
during times of prophesying and at other times as well.

The first two gifts help you to know what opened
the door for the demon or demons to enter the soul or
spirit, soul, and body. Through the manifestation of the
discerning of spirits, one has the ability to know what
demons are there. The discerning of spirits will allow
you to know if you are talking to the spirit being or to
the Spirit of God or to the devil himself when you are
engaged in conversation with the person. I walk with
all three revelation gifts: the word of wisdom, the word
of knowledge, and the discerning of spirits.

Kenneth E. Hagin believes the word of wisdom is the "best" gift. I contend that it depends on the ministry going forth. If the minister is conducting a deliverance session, then I believe the discerning of spirits is the most important gift because he or she will then be able to see if the evil spirit is in the person's soul or if the person is possessed of an evil spirit.

Often we may think discerning of spirits is simply a suspicion that a person or thing has a certain spirit when it's just our opinion. But if we have the gift, then we can be certain of whose voice we are hearing.

Discerning of spirits allows one to see into the spiritual realm. Acts 16:16–18 reveals:

> And it came to pass, as we went to prayer, a certain damsel possessed with a spirit of divination met us, which brought her masters much gain by soothsaying: The same followed Paul and us, and cried, saying, These men are the servants of the most high God, which show unto us the way of salvation. And this did she many days. But Paul, being grieved, turned and said to the spirit, I command thee in the name of Jesus Christ to come out of her. And he came out that same hour.

As you can see from the above passage, Paul was able to discern exactly what spirit (spirit of divination) was being carried by the young woman.

According to Kenneth E. Hagin, "God did not create the devil as he is now. We read in Ezekiel 28:15

that he was perfect until iniquity was found in him. God did not create him a devil. We read that he was lifted up because of his beauty (Ezekiel 28:17). We also read, in the beginning of time, before man was created, Satan ruled and had a kingdom. He said he would exalt his throne (Isaiah 13:13–14). It is possible that demons on the earth today could be the demons Satan ruled on the earth in the pre-Adamic kingdom. In my opinion, this is the case."[13]

As the Holy Spirit can manifest through those of us who have been filled with the Spirit of God, so do evil spirits want to embody Christians and non-Christians to be able to move and operate in the earth. Again Kenneth E. Hagin states,

> There is a spiritual gift called Discerning of Spirits. There is another gift called The Word of Knowledge that is really what some people call the Gift of Discernment—but it isn't. Too often what people call discernment is nothing but a 'gift' of suspicion and fault-finding. Too many have that gift. The true spiritual gift, Discerning of Spirits, has to do with spirits and not people. As Jesus said to me, 'Discerning of Spirits is supernatural insight into the realm of spirits.' One meaning of the word 'discern' is 'see'. Jesus told me I would be able to see in this realm and would see spirits. When the gift of Discerning of Spirits is in operation you will actually see into the realm of spirits.[14]

I have seen into the spiritual realm but not as strongly as Brother Hagin has. Of course, before he crossed over to the other side, he had walked this journey much longer than I. However, I have seen dark shadows pass by my bedroom door; and yes, I have felt their evil presence and smelled them. But I have not yet seen the images as Brother Hagin said that he has. Brother Hagin revealed his experience in seeing and dealing with demons in connection with his son-in-law.

So discerning of spirits is very important. With this gift, I reiterate, you will know if you are talking to the human being's spirit, the Holy Spirit, or a demon spirit. You will know when you are being lied to by a lying spirit, Praise God! So cry out to God and covet these gifts—the gift of the word of wisdom, gift of the word of knowledge, and of course, the gift of discerning of spirits. It is worth noting that the gift of discerning of spirits also allows us to see into the spiritual realm of light.

PERSONAL EXPERIENCE

One Friday evening as I lay on the sofa in my family room, I received an open vision. A navy blue coffin with a single red rosebud on it appeared before me. I began to ask God if this was a sign of my demise. However, I did not get an answer. I began to pray for everyone I could think of—my friends, my children, my grandchildren, my siblings, and of course, myself; but I still got no answer.

On Saturday morning I awakened with a burden to pray. I prayed until 12:40 p.m. when a phone call came from the church. I decided to stop praying and join the caller at the church. When I returned home, the burden to pray had lifted.

Sunday morning I noticed the answering machine was blinking. When I retrieved the message, a young woman's voice said, "Loreatha, come to mom's house; Dad just committed suicide." I felt really bad because I had stopped praying when I knew I was interceding for someone, even if I didn't know who it was. I was so upset and broken I couldn't bring myself to return her call on Sunday. Instead I went on to church and called her that Monday.

On Monday when I returned the call, she revealed that the death took place 1:00 p.m. on Saturday and went on to describe the details of the incident. She advised me that the family hour would be on Tuesday evening.

On Tuesday evening when I entered the funeral home, I was taken aback when I saw the navy blue coffin with a single red rosebud on it, just as I had seen in the vision. I contend that the discerning of spirits was in operation. Some may say it was the word of wisdom because it revealed the future death of a person. I had been ministering to him on a regular basis but had not spoken with him for several days. As far as I knew, I had done all that I knew to do. God doesn't always reveal the entirety of things. Sometimes He reveals in part. In the following chapter we will look at the methods of deliverance and the way the gifts of wisdom, knowledge, and discerning of spirits are used in deliverance.

CHAPTER 2
METHODS OF DELIVERANCE

HE FOLLOWING HEADINGS are some of the ways that deliverance comes to individuals:

DELIVERANCE BY FORGIVENESS

We can receive deliverance by reading the Word of God (Bible). If you carry unforgiveness and you read what God says about forgiveness you could get set free. God says if you do not forgive, I will not forgive you (Matt. 6:15). How often shall you forgive your brother?

> Then came Peter to him, and said, Lord, How often shall my brother sin against me, and I forgive him? till seven times? Jesus saith unto him, I say; not unto thee, Until seven times: but, until seventy times seven.
>
> —MATTHEW 18:21–22

Many times the spirit of unforgiveness will hide. It hid from me! I thought I had forgiven my children's father for the things of the past, but I had not forgiven him at all. God exposed His adversary—Satan. Really, it was not the devil but a demon of unforgiveness that had set up in my soul. There are many demons but only one devil, Satan.

Many times when preaching is going forth a person can get set free because "the word of God is quick, and powerful, and sharper than any twoedged sword, piercing even to the dividing asunder of soul and spirit" (Heb. 4:12). I remember one Sunday at my church, one of the elders said God spoke to her and wanted the congregation to forgive people and release them for whatever they were holding in unforgiveness. She also had us write it on paper and leave it at the altar; and we did. She explained if we did not forgive, God would not forgive us. Again, the Word penetrated the hearts and souls of the people and they were set free. There were some with "solid stone" faces, some had tears rolling down their cheeks, and others were crying aloud.

When Jesus responded to Peter, "I tell you, not seven times, but seventy-seven times" (Matt. 18:22, NIV), He was saying that every time someone sins against you, you should forgive him. He is not just talking about one who has come from the same womb when He speaks of forgiving your "brother." He is speaking of anyone born into this world—male or female. We must forgive if we want the Father (God) to forgive us.

Many times we are hurt so badly by another individual that we want to hold on to unforgiveness. Many times unforgiveness will hold on to us, even after the person dies. Unforgiveness can bring about physical problems. I did not develop physical problems while having unforgiveness for my children's father. I did not know I was a carrier of the demon of unforgiveness—not until I was in a church service and an evangelist prophesied to me that "God said you have unforgiveness in your heart for someone in your family and you are to forgive them now." I went back to my seat outdone, thinking she had missed it. However, a few weeks later I was talking to someone about my children's father and I felt the unforgiveness for him. God spoke to me and said, "That's who it is." So I said, "Father, the wounds are so deep. Please help me to forgive him." Because I remembered the Word of God and made the decision to forgive him, I was set free.

Dr. Don Colbert, a graduate of Oral Roberts School of Medicine, states:

> Forgiveness releases layers of hurt and heals the raw, jagged edges of emotional pain. It enables a person to release buried anger, resentment, bitterness, shame, grief, regret, guilt, hate and other toxic emotions that hide deep in the soul, making a person ill—both emotionally and physically. As a physician, I frequently treat people with physical problems that I feel are rooted in bitterness and unforgiveness.[1]

I agree with Dr. Colbert that all the things he mentioned that come through bitterness and unforgiveness are very deep-seated, with unforgiveness being the "strongman" causing all the other toxic things to set up a root of bitterness. Hebrews 12:15 says, "See to it that no one misses the grace of god and no bitter root grows up to cause trouble and defile many" (NIV).

You see, when unforgiveness is a part of one's life and if it is over a long period of time, a root of bitterness will and does set up in an individual's soul. After a while the thought of bitterness opens the door to the soul of the individual and a demon of bitterness enters and the person becomes a carrier of that spirit.

Dr. Colbert said further "Remember it is critically important to forgive yourself. If you cannot forgive yourself, you cannot forgive others."[2]

DELIVERANCE THROUGH TOUCH

After I had attended a conference in Grand Island, Nebraska, I discovered that I could, and still can, hug an individual and they will be delivered through that touch. I was told, "God is giving you authority in the spiritual realm and you want to move with caution. The demons watch you when you get up and when you lie down. You have real authority in the realm of darkness." I was told, "You shall see the dead arise." At that Grand Island conference a prophet came to me during the service and told me, "God told me to come and lay hands on you and release the apostolic mantle upon you. And from this day forward you will teach and will teach more prophetically." This was before I went before the seven prophets later that same night and they gave me the same message and much more.

I made two trips to Mexico with a pastor who takes teams into Mexico to minister. I made the trip in 2002 and 2003. He had the pastors preach and everyone else did testimonies and worked the altars. On these trips no one went just for the fun of it, although we had plenty of fun on the trips.

During the first trip, I gave testimonies and worked the altars at the different churches. However, on the second trip, I not only testified and worked the altar but also preached at a small church. While working the altar, I would hug the people at the altar and they would receive deliverance.

We went to an Indian family's house and the wife came out to greet us and we blessed her with Mexican money and prayed for her. I hugged her and she became very broken. I might add that over and over, when I hug a person, they will break down crying.

Deliverance through Prayer and Fasting

Deliverance comes by prayer and fasting. Mark 9 tells a story of a man with an evil spirit. It says, "When Jesus saw that a crowd was running to the scene, he rebuked the unclean spirit" (v. 25, NIV). The verse continues with Jesus speaking, saying, "You deaf and mute spirit,...I command you, come out of him and never enter him again" (NIV). Verse 26 tells us, "The spirit shrieked, convulsed the boy violently and came out. The boy looked so much like a corpse that many said, 'He's dead'" (NIV). Verses 27 and 28 tell us: "Jesus took him by the hand and lifted him to his feet and he stood up. After Jesus had gone indoors, his disciples asked him privately, 'Why they couldn't drive it out?'" (NIV). Jesus replied in verse 29: "This kind can come forth by nothing but by prayer and fasting."

I had a close friend who wanted me to minister to one of her children and their family. Whenever I would see the individual, we would always talk because she trusted me. I would tell her that the children had unforgiveness for their father, but the truth was always denied. One day my friend called me and said her son asked her to ask me to come and pray for him and his family. I told her that I would come. This was not a deaf and dumb spirit, but I suspected a spirit of unforgiveness so I fasted and prayed before the meeting. I was right. Her son was a carrier of unforgiveness for his father. The unforgiveness was not for what I thought it was. That's why it is important to minister what God gives you to minister. You should have focus only on what you are doing. We will discuss this in depth later on.

I want to reiterate that sometimes fasting and prayer are very much needed. The demons can be so deep-seated that the minister needs the Spirit of God to be able to manifest through him or her in a powerful way so that when the call comes in the name of Jesus to the demon to come out, they will come out without the minister going on for hours to get results.

CASTING OUT BY MINISTRY

Casting out demons by ministry is to begin praying. I like to begin praying in the Spirit (tongues); and then based on what I have discerned, that is where I begin to cast them out. I was called to come to a family's house because the two teenage brothers were fighting. When I arrived I found one brother was trying to keep the other brother from leaving home because the mother had asked him not to leave. The young man who was trying to leave was sitting on the bed in his room. When I asked him what was wrong, he did not respond. I sat on the end of the bed and began to pray in tongues and God began to speak to me and told me the "strongman" was bitterness.

I moved in front of him and began to call for the spirit of bitterness. And when I did, the spirit of bitterness (demon) came out of the young man and was foul. I said, "Did you see that?" Of course, you cannot see demons. But as I looked to my left where the young man's aunt was sitting, it had gone into her. I knew it had done this because the young lady's face took on a different form and she looked like she was frightened out of her mind. It was not her actions; it was the demon that had entered her. The reason it entered her was that her heart was not pure at the time. In other words, she had some things that she had not dealt with between her and another person. She was unclean; therefore, the demon was able to enter her. I then cast it out of her. During this process, both the young man and the aunt were set free.

Often as I am praying with the Spirit (tongues) or with my mind, God tells me what the individual is a carrier of (demons). I began to plead the blood of Jesus and call the demons by name and cast them out. It is not necessary to scream loudly; just speak normally and with authority and they will leave the person. They leave by tears (crying), coughing, vomiting, screaming, etc., as they leave the person. They may tear the person because they do not want to leave. They may speak to you, saying: (1) "Leave us alone," (2) "I don't want to leave," (3) "I'm not going to leave," or (4) they may cause the person to shake their heads, indicating they are not going to leave the person.

An unclean spirit may speak to the deliverance minister and accuse him or her of doing some sinful things, such as, "You know what I saw you doing last night." Whether it is true or not, they will sometimes make those kinds of accusations against the person who is doing the deliverance. It is simply a way of throwing the deliverance minister off track.

Jesus said in Matthew 12:

> When an evil spirit comes out of a man, it goes through arid places seeking rest and does not find it. Then it says, "I will return to the house

I left." When it arrives, it finds the house unoc-
cupied, swept clean and put in order. Then it
goes and takes with it seven other spirits more
wicked than itself, and they go in and live there.
And the final condition of that man is worse
than the first. That is how it will be with this
wicked generation.

—MATTHEW 12:43–45, NIV

As you can see, when the house is swept clean,
demons return to check the house in order to re-enter.
And when they do, they bring seven more demons
with them and things are worse than they were before.

The second time I was contacted about this young
man was on Halloween night when his brother called
me after my husband and I had gone to bed. He told
me his brother was speaking in an unknown tongue,
but he did not know if it was unknown tongues
inspired by the Holy Spirit or if it was of the devil. My
husband and I joined the brothers, the young man's
fiancée, and a friend. We met at a chosen location then
went to my house. After we arrived the mother joined
us, after which I began the deliverance process. After
the process had begun, the mother went and got her
brother to assist with the deliverance.

The young man with the spirit of bitterness as
the strongman had allowed the spirits to return and
things were worse than they were the first time. This
time, the spirits that were there were much stronger
and were accusatory and said, "Oh, you're not angry
this time," indicating that they remembered that the

last time I had become very angry and lost the control that I had come with. The mocking began in the form of laughing at me; telling me, "Yes, there are seven of us and we killed Him [Jesus] years ago." The young man had looked at the two pieces of jewelry (a cross and a pendant of a depiction of the head of Christ) that I was wearing when the aforementioned conversation took place. You never allow demons to speak unless you really need information to continue with the deliverance. In this case, I ordered the spirit speaking to me to shut up and began to cast all the unclean spirits out of the young man with the help of the mother's brother. On that night, once again, this young man was set free

I also learned on that night; when the manifestation is present, you can speak to the unclean spirits and tell them to "go down" so you can speak to the person who is the carrier of the evil spirit. You need to be able to, in all cases, communicate with the individual. I saw the second deliverance minister say to the demons, one by one, as he dealt with them to cast them out, "You go down right now," calling it by name. He may have had to say it a couple of times, but they would obey and go down. Then he was able to speak to the young man and tell him to denounce the demon. Once it was lust; once it was rejection and unforgiveness, etc. The young man was set free and filled with the Holy Spirit evidenced by speaking with other tongues.

WHO SHOULD AND SHOULD NOT RECEIVE DELIVERANCE

Everybody does not need deliverance. Those who do benefit from deliverance include: (1) Christian people who are saved, (2) infants in womb, (3) infants, (4) toddlers, (5) young children, (6) young adults, and (7) adults.

Christian people who are saved

People who have not received Christ as Savior (non-Christians who have not been born again) should not go through deliverance. The reason is because demons do look for a person who has been set free of demons so they can return to that person's soul and make them seven times worse than they were before. I don't recommend that non-believers go through deliverance without intentions of becoming a believer.

> When an evil spirit comes out of a man, it goes through arid places seeking rest and does not find it. Then it says, "I will return to the house I left." When it arrives, it finds the house unoccupied, swept clean and put in order. Then it goes and takes with it seven other spirits more wicked than itself, and they go in and live there. And the final condition of that man is worse than the first. That is how it will be with this wicked generation.
>
> —MATTHEW 12:43–45, NIV

I have taken non-Christians through deliverance and found they become worse off than they were before the deliverance. If he or she has not been born again (made Jesus Lord of their life), they are open to body, soul, and spirit being possessed by evil spirits. Christians who have a relationship with Christ can go through deliverance with a greater chance of remaining free from demons. However, even Christian people should be very careful once they have gone through deliverance, because the same thing can happen to them. They could possibly fall prey to attracting demons if they do not live and act a certain way. Chapter 5 discusses how to remain free of demons.

Infants in the womb

Inherited curses may give the devil the legal right to oppress, depress, and possess the human being. It can be at conception, while developing in the womb, or coming through the birth canal. God has decreed: "I the LORD thy God am a jealous God, visiting the iniquity of the fathers upon the children upon the third and fourth generation of them that hate me" (Deut. 5:9).

> Children are born with anywhere from few to many curses due to "the iniquities of the fathers," Exodus 20:5—parents, grandparents or great-grandparents have transgressed God's commandments, and the curse has been passed down. Perhaps there has been idolatry,

witchcraft, occult practices, incest, fornication, illegitimacy, adultery, bestiality or other transgressions in the family tree. Unless these curses have already been disallowed, the atoning blood of Jesus accepted, and the demons of curse expelled, then the devil has a right to perpetuate the curse to another generation.[3]

At conception the baby needs to be wanted and loved while it is in the womb. The baby should be prayed for in the womb and generational curses broken off of him or her. A young lady was threatening a miscarriage and was hospitalized. I went to pray for her and her sister-in-law was there. I prayed for the sister-in-law also. As I lay my hands on her abdomen, she began to cough and throw up. I believe generational curses were being broken off from her baby and the evil spirits left.

In addition, mothers can have addictions that can be passed on to the baby in the womb. When the baby is born, it may go through withdrawals because the drugs are no longer passing from the mother to the baby. Often later in life or sometimes early in their life the person begins to use drugs (crack, cocaine, alcohol, etc.). Sometimes the addiction comes down through the bloodlines. One of my nurses told me her son has not seen his father since he was two years old. However, he is sixteen now and he walks like him, talks like him, and uses alcohol like the father. Many times the person needs deliverance to get past these addictions. If we build a relationship with Christ, we can and will be set free from addictions.

Infants

Infants must be protected from Satan and his demons. The mother should never leave her baby anywhere for a long period of time. The spirit of abandonment, rejection, and not being loved could possibly enter the infant. As the child grows up, you will see unexplained anger.

Toddlers

Toddlers are to be protected. Parents should not leave them with people who are not well known. I worked deliverance with a woman who was molested at four years of age. In her late forties it was still affecting her marriage. She was a carrier of shame and of a spirit of perversion. They dwelt in her subconscious. When her brother told about his molestation, that caused her to remember her own violation at four years of age. She was set free by the deliverance team.

Young children

Jesus let us know that not only adults but also children may have deliverance needs.

> But Jesus said unto her, Let the children first be filled: for it is not meet to take the children's bread, and to cast it unto the dogs....And he said unto her, For this saying go thy way; the devil is gone out of thy daughter.
>
> —MARK 7:27, 29

Mark 16:17 reads, "And these signs shall follow them that believe; In my name shall they cast out devils."

When Jesus came down from the Mount of Transfiguration, He found His disciples had failed to minister deliverance to a young boy.

And one of the multitude answered and said, Master, I have brought unto thee my son, which hath a dumb spirit; And wheresoever he taketh him, he teareth him; and he foameth, and gnasheth with his teeth, and pineth away: and I spake to thy disciples that they should cast him out; and they could not. He answereth him, and saith, O faithless generation, how long shall I be with you? And how long shall I suffer you? Bring him unto me. And they brought him unto him: and when he saw him, straightway the spirit tare him; and he fell on the ground, and wallowed foaming. And he asked his father, how long is it ago since this came unto him; and he said, of a child. And ofttimes it hath cast him into the fire, and into the waters, to destroy him: but if thou canst do anything, have compassion on us, and help us. Jesus said unto him, 'If though canst believe, all things are possible to him that believeth.' And straightway the father of the child cried out, and said with tears, Lord, I believe; help thou mine unbelief. When Jesus saw that the people came running together, he rebuked the foul spirit, saying unto him, Thou dumb and deaf spirit, I charge thee, come out of him, and enter no more into him. And the spirit cried, and rent him sore, and came of him: and he was as one dead; insomuch that many said,

He is dead. But Jesus took him by the hand, and lifted him up; and he arose. And when he was come into the house, his disciples asked him privately, why could not we cast him out? And he said unto them, This kind can come forth by nothing, but by prayer and fasting.

—MARK 9:17–29

Bill Banks in his book *Deliverance for Children & Teens* explains the former scripture:

Jesus left the blueprint to deliverance for children: Mark 9:17–29...shows deliverance for young people as well as for adults. Jesus also showed that there is no distance in prayer and sometimes you may need to fast and pray. On this particular occasion of ministry to a child, we noticed a number of steps.

He received a *presentation of the candidate's need* described by an observer in verse 17.

Jesus utilized *a description of the candidate's behavior* by a close relative, when perhaps the subject could not speak for himself, verses 17, 18.

He apparently utilized *physical observation* of the candidate for deliverance in verse 20. When closely observed, demons get stirred up and sometimes manifest themselves violently.

Jesus also employed the *inquiry method* in verse 21, asking questions to determine when the demon first manifested, in order to determine when it had entered the boy.

Jesus offers encouragement for faith to believe, assures that the deliverance was both possible and at hand, verse 23.

He *rebuked the spirit by name*—this was obvious even to the parent because it caused the child to be unable to speak (verse 25).

He apparently *received and utilized a revelation*, in rebuking also a deaf spirit-verse 25.

He *spoke the command* to come out and to never enter again in verse 25.

The spirit's reaction was violent, either manifesting or attempting to camouflage itself as a spirit of death in verse 26.

When a root (strongman) spirit is discerned and threatened with expulsion, it will often try to deter the one ministering with fearful actions, in this particular case by manifesting itself as death.[4]

When I was a young Christian and new to performing deliverance, the following incident took place: a young woman with whom I was working fell to the floor as "stiff as a board." Fear did not come upon me. As a new Christian, I was very childlike. Whatever the Bible said, I could do; I went forth in it without doubt or fear. The Bible said I could cast out devils, and so that's what I did. As she fell to the floor, I went to the floor with her. I said then, "In the name of Jesus Christ, you cocaine spirit, come out of her!" She screamed very loudly as the spirit was leaving her and she became free at that same hour.

Still referring to Mark 9:17–29, Bill Banks continues:

Jesus in addition employed *a healing touch* to lift the boy, in verse 27, and then the boy was able to arise himself. It was Jesus' power (strength) that lifted the boy, just as Peter's strength lifted the cripple in Acts 3. After the cripple was on his feet, as a result of the action of Peter, "his feet and ankle bones received strength." Luke 9:42b explains that Jesus rebuked the unclean spirit and healed the young child and delivered him unto his father.[5]

Bill Banks then states:

> Jesus responded to the disciples' question regarding their impotency by explaining that "this kind (strongly entrenched, long established spirit, which had bridged the gap from the spirit to other physical realm, in order to physically manifest freely and powerfully in the boy's life) can only come forth by prayer and fasting." Thus, He indicates that the *one ministering needs to prepare himself* for spiritual battles *in advance*, by means of prayer and fasting, verse 29.[6]

The only time I have read in Scripture where Jesus did interviewing was in the case of the possessed man at Gadara. Unless there is an "on the spot" manifestation, I always interview the candidate for deliverance. It is different with young children; you should interview the mother first and then interview the child. You will then get a better understanding of what spirits the child is carrying.

I worked with a young boy who we will call Jim. The father convinced the mother, who lived in another state, that she should leave Jim with him in Nebraska rather than having him travel back home with her. The father told the mother it would be difficult for her to travel with him and his older brother, so she left him with the father who promised to bring Jim to her later. The mother did not get Jim back until years later. The mother had to go through the courts to get custody of her son.

Things went well for awhile after getting her son back. Jim appeared to be a sweet little eight-year-old boy. The grandmother began to tell me about Jim's behavior. She told me he was having sudden outbursts of anger. I found that hard to believe, because when I was around him he was so respectful. I was told he would hit his brother for no reason. He hit the brother at the child care center and the caregiver attempted to put him in a time out. Jim refused to go into time out. The mother disciplined Jim for his disobedience

A few days later the grandmother called me in to take Jim through deliverance (after getting approval from the mother). They had been at a local store when Jim hit his brother. When the grandmother tried to discipline Jim, he kicked her. The mother, grandmother, oldest brother, and the mother's pastor were present. I interviewed the mother and grandmother first. Secondly, I asked the nine-year-old brother a few questions. Lastly, I interviewed Jim. I asked him if he remembered his mother leaving him and his answer was no. He was only two years old when she left him.

The pastor began to weep. He said, "I saw Jim in a corner crying." I then asked Jim why he kicked his grandmother. He said, "The evil part of mind told me to do it." Because spirits can be transferable, I asked the brother to leave the room. I asked the mother to ask Jim to forgive her for abandoning him. I advised her to tell him how much she loves him. As the mother shared her love with her son, he began to cry. The mother also began to cry as she told him of her love. I bound up the spirit of anger and abandonment and cast them out. Tears rolled down his cheeks. I asked him if he knew why he was crying. He answered, "No," as tears rolled down his face. He was set free and I released the anointing and peace of God upon him. Today he lives a peaceful and an obedient life with his mother, brother, and grandmother.

I haven't worked with children very often. However, I found the authority is the same as with adults. You have the authority and the demons must obey. Even children know when they need prayer.

All physical conditions in children are not of the body but sometimes they are because demons are present. Luke 13:11 talks about a crippled woman whom Jesus set free by casting out the spirit of infirmity. The Holy Spirit, in the name of Jesus, will also set children free.

Some ministers feel that you should not allow the child to touch the parent(s) during deliverance. They feel that it prolongs the deliverance and that the demons are able to stay longer. So, it is thought to keep a small child on your lap or close to you. Also, tell the parent(s) not to interfere. The child will sometimes reach for the parent(s). It is good to have the parent(s) present in case you have questions. Children also can be set free from demon harassment.

Young adults

I have worked with a great number of young adults. They seem to have many problems with the following spirits:

- Lust
- Perversion (masturbation, oral sex, pornography)
- Rejection
- Anger
- Depression
- Suicide
- Molestation
- Rape
- Abandonment

Young people usually come to me for counseling, but you do not counsel demons. Some of the young people are married and need help. One such couple I will call Mary and James. They sought help because the wife was committing adultery. These were very young adults—twenty and twenty-three. James was all but begging her to change her ways. She was very controlling. She was a Jezebel; and where there is a Jezebel, there is an Ahab. In the Bible, Jezebel was Ahab's wife but she controlled him. Jezebel gave Ahab orders. She would tell him to "jump" and he would ask, "How high?" In 1 Kings 19:1–2 it says, "Ahab told Jezebel all that Elijah had done, and withal how he had slain all the prophets with the sword. Then Jezebel sent a message unto Elijah, saying, So let the gods do to me, and more also, if I make not thy life as the life of one of them by tomorrow about this time." Ahab was the king, but Jezebel ran things.

As I interviewed the wife, I discovered she had been molested. She had been abandoned when she was very young and her grandmother raised her. So I dealt with the controlling spirit (Jezebel), molestation (shame), rejection, and abandonment. She was set free. The husband was set free of the spirit of Ahab.

Adults

There was an instance of adult deliverance involving another couple. This couple was engaged to be married. The young man and I went on a trip to a conference. On the return trip to Omaha, we discussed his potential wedding.

We talked about issues that might surface. These issues included addiction, the fact that they were members of separate churches, and receiving premarital counseling. Nothing was solved, and the marriage took place. A few months later he had returned to an addiction. The demons began to rage. I only worked with him once, and he was not set free. He did not really want freedom from his addiction.

The wife went through deliverance and received freedom from rejection, hurt, and loneliness. She needed a stronger relationship with God, which she pursued. Today she is very strong young woman in Christ. She is able to parent her children because she is free from evil spirits. Also she was able to get a very good job.

I have worked with many adults and they, all except two, were confessing Christians. The two non-Christians were done before I received revelation not to deliver non-Christians because they would become worse than they were before the deliverance. My *first goal* is to lead them to Christ. One young man was worse than before. I know he became worse because the demons began talking to me during the second deliverance. I told them to "shut up" and cast them out.

Not every Christian needs deliverance, but it is possible every non-Christian needs deliverance—the reason being they are in darkness and are in need of the marvelous light. They are in danger of soul, body, and spirit being controlled by their master, Satan.

Frank Hammonds relates a story of when he was at a Full Gospel Business Men's meeting. There was a large group of "hippies" in the back of the auditorium. He said,

> As I looked at the first fellow a pain struck me in the stomach as though I had been hit with a fist.

> Turning to a stranger sitting next to me, I whispered, "Is that man in the Spirit of the Lord?" He replied, "I don't know but he surely don't look good." "Why, he has a demon!" I exclaimed. The brother next to me suggested, "Perhaps you have a gift of discernment." With assurance that I could not account for, I said, "I don't know what I have, but I know what he had. He has a demon!" Now the gifts of the Spirit were relatively unknown to me at that time, and I had learned nothing about demon spirits.[7]

Three of the "hippies" headed for the microphone in front when Hammond discerned the evil spirit. When they reached the microphone, the one with the demon said, "I am the way; I am Jesus."[8] Needless to say, they cast the familiar spirit out of the young man.

Deliverance can be needed from the time of conception through adulthood

THE HOW AND WHEN OF DELIVERANCE

The deliverance sessions begins with an interview with the individual. The deliverance session differs only when you work with a child. With the adult, I always interview them *first* to determine what demons they are carrying. It does not matter whether it is a man or a woman as to how I screen them in the process of getting them ready to go through deliverance.

Usually I will begin by telling the person who I am and make small talk. Then the interview begins:

How old are you?

Are you married?

How long have you been married?

Do you have children?

Are your parents still alive?

How was your childhood?

Review the person's adulthood.

Has the person been married?

Are you married?

If married, are you happily married?

Many times they will answer that their childhood was great and/or their marriage was great, but God will show me it was a "mess": for example, the mother working two jobs to make ends meet and sometimes there is no father in the household; or there is a favorite in the household, favored by mom or dad, and I find rivalry between the siblings. Once I discern by the Holy Spirit what demons the person is carrying, the deliverance begins.

The same process is for children. However, things for children are a little different because you need to ask the parents a lot of questions about the child:

What was the pregnancy like?

What was the delivery like?

Did you have to leave the child at the hospital because it was premature?

If there are other children, you ask if they compare the children to each other.

You may ask all these questions and more because you are trying to discern by the Holy Spirit what demon the child is carrying. I might add that some pregnant mothers need to have their unborn prayed over.

Once when I was praying for a young lady who was having complications from pregnancy, there was another young woman there who was also pregnant. I laid hands on her abdomen and began to break curses off of the baby and the mother began to vomit. I believe the baby was delivered of family curses.

There have been a few times I did not have the chance to interview. Even so, when the demons manifested, I began to, with the Holy Spirit, get them set free from the demons they were carrying.

CHAPTER 3
MY EXPERIENCES IN DELIVERANCE

2001 conference trip to Chicago

In chapter 4 in "My Call to Deliverance Ministry," there is discussion pertaining to the deliverance that took place following a Chicago conference trip.

2002 experiences

I was on the telephone with my fiancé. He told me I had to take him like he was, and I told him I was done because he was a Mason. I had decided to end the relationship because of my understanding that Freemasonry is a cult and for me that is outside of the principles of God.

A call came from a young lady's house and her oldest son and the next oldest were having a negative confrontation. They wanted me to come help handle the situation. I went to the young lady's house in my pajamas. When I arrived, the mother, the son, and the aunt were in the son's room. He was sitting on the bed. His mother was standing in front of him, and his aunt was sitting by him on the bed. When I sat at the end of the bed and began to pray in other tongues, God told me there was another influence that was affecting the young man's behavior. I stood up in front of the young man and began to call for deliverance of rejection and rebellion. When I called for bitterness, that spirit came out and I thought it went out of the window; but it had entered the aunt! I looked at her and asked, "Did you see that?" The demon had entered her. I then cast it out of her. As I kept on with the deliverance, I got angry and I lost the focus of my authority. The demons began to make fun of me—laughing and mocking. The mother went to get her brother because I had lost control. He came and took authority. He commanded them to "go down" so he could speak to the young man and have him to forgive his mom. He felt his mom did not love him because she was having a lot of children. He had animosity toward his siblings because he felt they were taking his place. He had to forgive his biological father, his step-father, and step-sister. His uncle called for lust demons, stupid spirit, spirit of failure, and spirit of fear. He then led him into salvation and the baptism of the Holy Spirit with the evidence of tongues. I took the son home with me and played worship music all night in my prayer room. The next day he told me he was able to see naturally. Things even looked different to him, and he could think clearly. However, he needed to be delivered again in 2003.

I met a woman at the Salvation Army. Her mother had died while she and her sister were very young. They both grew up with their father after he was awarded custody in a court battle. The father was disabled and the girls took the wrong path of life. This woman was the oldest of the siblings and had become addicted to drugs and promiscuity. She was angry because her mother had died and left her. She was angry with the father for being abusive to the mother while she was alive. So when I met her, she was still dealing with all these issues. I prayed with her for salvation and took her through deliverance and she was set free.

2003 experiences

My mentee called me and said she had some problems. I picked her up at her house and took her to breakfast at a local restaurant. As I spoke to her about her situation, she wept uncontrollably. I told her she needed deliverance, and she agreed with me. She had stolen from stores since her youth. She stated she did not know why. It was not just for survival but the fact she felt good when she got away with it. There would be a rush of satisfaction when she stole. We returned to her house and went to the basement. I began the deliverance with her childhood and worked my way through to her adulthood. I called for a kleptomaniac spirit, rejection spirit, the spirit of perfectionism, and spirit of perversion. Then I prayed for the peace of God and released the spirit of love upon her and anointing. The mentee was set free of stealing. She loves God but she had no control.

2004 experience during training

During training we practiced with each other. The pastor was the teacher. I was very reluctant to deliver anyone; I felt that in that kind of environment I would not be able to be effective. The team and I were working together during the training. One of the team members could not deliver one of the other team members because he was her nephew. She asked me to do it. I hesitated because I did not like the environment where you are searching for demons and assuming everyone is a carrier of demons. I was tired; and I am more careful going forth in deliverance when I am physically exhausted, sick, upset, or angry. It causes one to lose focus and does no one any good. I don't know why she didn't want to work with her nephew. To work on a family member is to your advantage. It is not like prophesying. You're not giving a prophetic word and you do have to be afraid of saying what you know. Many times you can go after what you have seen through the Spirit of God and what you have seen set up over a period of time. It could be friend or family.

Deliverance of a relative:

I attempted deliverance with the nephew and failed. I believe I failed because:

I was reluctant.

I was fatigued.

I was agitated.

I am not sure what was bothering me. I searched myself to see if I needed deliverance but was never sure because it had been a long time since I worked on myself. I asked the nephew if he was having bad dreams. I discerned that he had nightmares. He said that he did.

He dreamed about things chasing him, things like skeletons. He named other things that I do not remember. So I asked him if he watched "scary" movies. He said that he did. I told him he should not watch those movies because the content can enter into his soul. Then I began the deliverance. I called up the spirit of torment.

It was difficult to be able to listen to God for what happened next. The aunt began to call certain things for me to call out for deliverance; and that was a deterrent for me to continue with the deliverance. Teamwork is good if there is more than one deliverance minister. He or she should make the command. In other words, one person at a time should make the command. If the other ministers discern something, they should ask if they can take command and begin deliverance. While one minister is working the other, one is praying softly unless the ministering person begins praying in tongues. Always follow the lead of the person in command. When the aunt started telling me to call all these different things (spirits), then I could not go forth with discerning of spirits because she caused me to lose my focus. I told her I had to stop, and she requested another team member to take up where I left off. Then they felt like they were successful with deliverance of the nephew. Again the team member was told by the aunt what to call out. I looked on but was troubled because the nephew was looking from the aunt to the team member. Not often, but every now and then, he would look away from the team member to his aunt who was telling the team member what spirits to call out. This had caused the young man to become confused.

The aunt then began deliverance on one of the team members. (The aunt was not just his aunt but was an elder in the church.) She began to call for the spirit of defiance and unforgiveness. I discerned that she had forgiven her husband but the hurt from rejection was what had set up in her soul. I asked the aunt if I could call for those spirits that I had discerned, and she said yes. Therefore, she gave me permission to go forth with deliverance. I began to call for the spirit of hurt and rejection, and there was a manifestation. I was able to cast out the demon of hurt and the demon of rejection.

Other experiences

One of my mentees called me and said a friend of hers was at her house and asked me if I could come there. The mentee said, "She needs deliverance big-time." I told her I would come to her house, and I went. The friend was attempting to leave when I arrived. I asked if I could pray for her. At first, she reluctantly agreed. We went inside and I began to pray. As I always do, I tapped into the gift of knowledge and the word of wisdom. I began to ask questions based on what the Holy Spirit was showing me. I asked about her children and her childhood, and I found she had lost her children through the courts. As a child, she was a triplet and the only survivor. Her mother did not know who their father was. I was told the mother stabbed herself in the stomach to kill the triplets, and she survived. When she was sixteen years old, her brother raped her. The mother knew of the incest but denied that it ever happened. I began the deliverance process by calling up the spirits of rejection, bitterness, abandonment, hurt, and unforgiveness. Things went well for awhile. She was rocking back and forth and crying. She went near to my mentee to be able to draw strength to continue. I not only believe it was for her to draw strength but also for the evil spirits to draw strength to remain in her. At my request, the mentee did not allow any physical contact. The friend rose to her feet. A demon began to say, "Don't push." That came right after I was leading her to call on Jesus. I then dealt with the spirit of bondage, so she could speak. The friend began saying softly, "Jesus, help me." I had commanded all spirits to "go down" so I could speak to her. Again, the demon (through the friend) began to say, "Don't push. I'm telling you, don't push."

While the demons were down, I had her to renounce

them; then I called them back up to cast them out, but she had no control to help release the demons. I was forced to leave her bound. When she knelt in front of me, she stated, "I know you are anointed. I feel the Holy Spirit coming from you." I don't believe it was the individual who was speaking to me, but believe it was one of the spirits. This happened to Jesus when He went to Gadara and the demons asked Him if He was coming to trouble them before it was time (Matt. 8:29).

This same mentee that had me over for the friend, had met with me before this time. I also took her through a process of deliverance. I met her after she was released from jail. She was determined to be set free. I remember it was a beautiful sunshiny day. The mentee was hurting and ready to turn her life around. I interviewed her by asking about her childhood and her adulthood. The gift of the word of wisdom and the gift of the word of knowledge began to surface. The mentee had been molested at an early age, allowing the spirits of perversion, rejection, unforgiveness, and pride (I can do it all by myself) set up in her. Her children were in foster care and the relationship with her mother was nonexistent. The process of deliverance took place, and she was set free of all demonic activity.

Another experience involved activation after verbal teaching on the prophetic. There was a man named Joe who had lost his wife. This information did not surface until the pastor blessed him with a prophetic word from God. The pastor prayed for him and asked everyone to extend their hands toward him. I went over and laid hands on him. Others did the same. When the pastor prayed, Joe almost manifested. I could smell the demons, just as in other instances where I smelled them. However, I did nothing because I was not in charge of the prayer.

A pastor and wife were visiting a local church when the wife was called out for a prophetic word. She stood in front of the pastor. He told her that God was going to bless her and restore what the devil had taken from her. Hands were laid on her, and she went down to the floor. Her body began to vibrate with her feet beating against the floor. Her body also began to rise all the way up from the floor from her waist to her head. I knelt down by her and so did another team member, and we began to pray. We were not ministering deliverance but just praying for her. The co-pastor told us to cease praying, and we did just that. A pastor from another local church came over and began to pray a prayer of deliverance, and I prayed with her. She was set free from whatever spirits she was carrying.

I have had experiences with tangible manifestations. With some deliverances the manifestation may be very strong, yet another time there may not be any manifestation at all. If there are none, then ask the person to breathe in and out several times. Whatever spirits you have discerned and have bound and attempted to cast out, do what I call a "dry run" (calling them by name) to see if they hid from you. For example, if you have called for the spirit of fear, you will call for fear again to see if you get a reaction to the call. During a deliverance session a while back, after I had called for different demons and fear was one of them, I made the "dry run" and called for the spirit of fear. The fear spirit had pretended to have left the person. I recognized it was still there when she started to cough and gag. I proceeded to cast it out.

Sometimes the demons want to hold a conversation with you. This is another example of verbalization. Do not talk to them except to cast them out unless you need to know the names of the demons that are in the person. Of course, you may want them to go down so you can speak to the person. When you order them to "go down" you are causing the manifestation to stop. You are then able to talk to the person, ask him or her questions, and give directions. You may ask the person what spirits they think they have. Whether you discern it or the person tells you what evil spirits are present, you can have the person being delivered to renounce each demon. Once they have been renounced, you may cast them out. After that you call them back up (start the manifestation again). Other manifestations may surface during delivery. Demon manifestation can appear in many different ways.

I remember before my church moved from our last location, we had a young evangelist come to run a spiritual meeting. He was very anointed. He made an altar call for people to come up to the front for prayer to break the spirit of astrology from their lives. Astrology is a group of beliefs in which knowledge of the positions of celestial bodies is thought to be helpful in understanding our daily lives and our earthly affairs. People often check astrology to see if they are going to have a great love affair in the future, etc.

When the pastor looked around to see if there was anyone else coming to the altar, a lady began to look back. I wondered what she was looking at, so I looked back also to see nothing. She began to walk towards the young minister, and he happened to look her in the face and he said, "Get me the oil." When she reached him, he anointed her head with oil. Full manifestation came and her face became more and more distorted as she approached the pastor. The demon began to speak, and it took five men to hold the seventy-year-old woman down. The voice was very strong, heavy, and masculine sounding. This woman not only was seventy years old or older, but she probably weighed one hundred thirty pounds "soaking wet!" But she was set free.

Odors are another way demons manifest. I smelled a foul odor with the young homosexual man who was in the hospital and another instance at a local restaurant. Then there was the man who had failed to grieve for his wife, and I smelled the demon of guilt and torment. This one smelled like he needed a good shower after a couple of weeks without a shower.

A spirit of pride may cause the person to sit or walk in a certain manner or hold their heads kind of up in the air. Matthew 8:29 tells us how demons will cry out in manifestation. The Scripture reads, "What have we to do with thee, Jesus, thou Son of God? art thou come hither to torment us before the time?" This scripture proves they will manifest and will speak to you. But Jesus did not allow them to speak.

In addition to the examples above, there are other ways that demons may manifest. They include: (1) regurgitation of matter that is not necessarily food but a foamy looking substance, (2) coughing, (3) crying, (4) yawning, and (5) screaming.

CHAPTER 4

THE DELIVERANCE MINISTER

KNOWING YOUR AUTHORITY IN THE REALM OF DARKNESS

We do have authority in the earth and in the realm of darkness. In Luke 10:19 Jesus says, "Behold, I give unto you power to tread on serpents and scorpions, and over all the power of the enemy: and nothing shall by any means hurt you."

Also I want you to look again at Mark 16:17 where Jesus states, "And these signs shall follow them that believe; In my name shall they cast out devils." Evidently the sons of Sceva, a Jew, and chief of the priests did not understand their authority because they said to them who had evil spirits, "We adjure you by Jesus whom Paul preacheth" (Acts 19:13). They did not say it with authority as in, "You foul or you unclean spirit, come out in the name of Jesus." It was evident they were not believers. As a result, deliverance did not occur and they were chased down the street naked and wounded.

Sometimes if you are not living right, the demons will talk about you and expose the wrongdoings in your life while you are attempting to do ministry.

REMOVING THE SPIRIT OF BONDAGE

The deliverance minister should make it known to the individual who is receiving deliverance that the commands that will be spoken during the session will not be directed to or at them. There are times the demon may speak; and as Jesus did, you will command them to be quiet and come out of the person. The minister may tell the demon to shut up and go down so he or she can speak to the receiver. After the minister has given directions to the receiver, he or she will call the demon back up and cast it out. The direction may be to renounce the spirits that have been discerned to be in the soul.

These are things the Holy Spirit taught me after the following experience in York, Nebraska:

In the 1980s while on a trip to the women's prison complex in York, Nebraska, under the leadership of a dear friend, I began to pray for a young woman.

First, let me go back and share an open vision that was given to me while I was at work at Fort Calhoun, Nebraska, as a nuclear plant guard. While I was working the access lanes in the nuclear facility, I had an open vision, wherein the giant window began to fill in like a large television screen. I saw a woman in a tan uniform on this screen. I asked God, "Who is she?" But I received no answer.

When the church I was with made the trip to the prison and before service started, I saw the young woman that I had seen in the vision! I asked who she was, and I was told. She had not been there very long. After the service ended I went to her and began to minister to her. I discovered she was addicted to crack cocaine and that she wanted to be free. I began to pray for her. Then I sensed I was to cast out the cocaine demon, so I said, "I bind you up, you cocaine demon, and I cast you out." When I said that, she became "stiff as a board" and fell to the floor. I went down with her. As I went down I heard, "Jesus I know and Paul I know, but who are you?" Then I heard, "Call it [the spirit demon] by name and cast it out." So again I said, "Come out of her you cocaine demon." She screamed loudly and was freed that same hour. My friend and some of the praise team members were in the kitchen right outside the chapel. When they heard the scream, they came running into the chapel.

During the ride back to Omaha, I heard the Father say, "You will never hear that again: 'Jesus I know and Paul I know, but who are you?'" I have not heard it again, and that was many years before God promoted me to deliverance minister.

In 2001 God opened the door to the realm of

darkness and gave me total authority to cast out demons. I would like to introduce you to ways deliverance comes to an individual.

SETTING THE CAPTIVES FREE

Deliverance took place in 1995 in my former church. It happened after church one Sunday. One of the ministers and his wife asked me to pray for their daughter. I began to pray for her, knowing demons were present. As I tried to get her to say, "Jesus is Lord," she could not speak. It was like something was holding her mouth together. I believe the Holy Spirit revealed to me that the spirit of bondage was holding her hostage. Romans 8:15 tell us, "For ye have not received the spirit of bondage again to fear; but ye have received the Spirit of adoption, whereby we cry, Abba, Father."

I had not been given full authority in the realm of darkness. However, in Mark 16:17 Jesus says, "And these signs shall follow them who believe: In my name shall they cast out devils; they shall speak with new tongues." So I was still covered by the blood of Jesus. I called the church pastor over because it did not seem like things were moving very fast; but after his reinforcement, she was set free.

The word began to spread and people began to ask for me to pray for them to be set free. A young woman (not a member of our church) came to me one Sunday morning and asked for me. Someone had told her to look me up. Needless to say, God set her free.

PREPARING FOR DELIVERANCE

Do not go while angry.

Do not go to do a deliverance session or do deliverance while you are angry. In other words, you should not be walking in any sin. I know and understand that God knows we are going to get angry from time to time. However, God tells us to be angry and sin not: "Be ye angry, and sin not, let not the sun go down upon your wrath: neither give place to the devil" (Eph. 4:26–27). In this scripture, God is not suggesting that we get past anger; He is commanding that we get past anger and sin not and that we leave no place for the enemy (Satan) to bring sin into our lives.

Do not get angry in the midst of doing deliverance.

Once I went in anger and became more angered during the delivery. I received a call to come and perform deliverance on a young man, and I was unprepared. I had strong disagreement with an individual just before the call came in. I left my house very upset from the previous telephone conversation.

I started the process of deliverance with the young man, and I became very angry. Now I was not just upset from the phone conversation but had become angry at the demons that were holding the young man captive. It is worth noting here that the young man was a very close relative of mine and that is why I got angry because the demons were not leaving him as fast as I desired. It is important that you understand that you do not go to perform deliverance while you are angry or become angry while you are casting out demons. You will lose your control or authority if you do so. Perhaps I should say it like this: your authority "goes out of the window."

Demons and the devil are not omnipresent as God is; however, the demons that had him possessed began to talk about the things that were said in an earlier telephone conversation that had angered me.

Tonight God revealed to me as I began to write about the account that an angry spirit had ridden with me to the young man's house. That's why the demons could repeat things that were said. Because I had lost control, my authority in the spiritual realm of darkness had been weakened. Due to my anger, the demons began to mock me. Another person was called in to continue the deliverance and the young man was set free.

Be healthy, not sick.

You must be healthy. You must not be ill when participating or performing deliverance. If so, you will leave yourself open for demons to enter your soul. I joined a deliverance team to work with a young man who was dealing with the spirit of pornography. In addition, during the deliverance, it was revealed that as a young boy he had been sexually abused and made to keep it a secret.

A couple of weeks following this deliverance I was on an emotional roller coaster. I had things going on with my children and step-children that had brought a lot of stress and depression upon me. I had left myself open for demons to oppress me. Depression was so strongly attached to me, I felt like I was losing my mind. My mentor called me "out of the blue" just to check on me. I said I needed to talk with her. She came and picked me up the same day. We went out to eat, and she told me she could see depression all over me. After we had finished eating, we went to the church where she was co-pastor with her husband and she was able to break the spirit of depression from me. During this time, the minister of music played worship songs.

Before my mentor called me, I had called pastors whom I knew walked in deliverance, but they were out of town. When they returned they called me to see if I still wanted to meet. I started to decline; but I was not strong yet, even though my mentor had set me free. I went and received prayer from them. I believe that helped to restore my strength in the Lord.

Have no fear.

Second Timothy 1:7 says, "God hath not given us the spirit of fear; but of power, and of love, and of a sound mind." You must know who you are in Christ. You must know you have authority in the realm of darkness. You must be led by the Holy Spirit. You must overcome fear. Many people stay away from deliverance because of fear. I no longer walked in fear because Jesus cast out demons. First John 3:8 tells us that Jesus came into the world to destroy the works of Satan. When He prayed to the Father for the Comforter to come to us (the Holy Spirit), He gave all power to the people of God to deal with the realm of darkness. He gave them power to go in and tear down the demons' nesting place in the human being and in the atmosphere.

When you come against demons with the authority of Jesus Christ and with the power of His shed blood, all demons must obey your command. Very few churches teach the subject of deliverance; therefore, it seems to me most deliverance ministers stumble into the ministry as I did. Of course, I had read where Jesus said that we (Christians) could do the same thing He did when He walked the earth (John 14:12); so when I was confronted with setting a person free, I walked in deliverance.

Satan is the father of lies. John 8:44 tells us he is. He will come to you with threats, but do not listen. The threats include attacking your health or your family and friends with sickness and death. But go forward in your ministry. God tells us in Luke 10:19 that "nothing shall by any means hurt you." Satan will also come against you with lies through other people. I have had people to indicate that all I think about is the kingdom of darkness and that I'm incapable of serving in any other area of the kingdom. I do walk very strongly in deliverance; however, God has blessed me with many other gifts. I believe a church should be well rounded. It should operate under *all* of God's principles, not some of His principles. He would not have given us the discerning of spirits if He had not wanted us to destroy the kingdom of Beelzebub.

Pigs in the Parlor by Frank and Ida Mae Hammond states,

> A few pastors whom I know, started out in deliverance ministry and the Devil told them that they would lose members or that prospective members would be frightened away. Undoubtedly, the Devil will cause some to be offended or afraid. But when a pastor begins to guard his own little kingdom at the expense of disobeying Christ's commission, he will lose much more than he had hoped to gain.[1]

The Hammonds also emphasized how Satan will use other people to try and discourage or bring fear to you so you will back off of getting people set free from the clutches of the devil.

> Have you heard that pastor so-and-so is casting demons out of Christians? If the devil cannot defeat you with fear tactics and lies, he will resort to criticism in the mouths of others. Two ministers were talking; the first one said, "We have to be very careful these days about false doctrine and false teachers. Why have you heard that some preacher by the name of Hammond is going around in our area casting demons out of Christians?" The second minister passed up the opportunity of saying, "Hammond is ministering deliverance to my own flock right now.

All Hammond ever thinks about is the Devil. I believe we should just keep our minds on Jesus."[2]

Hammond responds to this kind of statement by saying "My, the Devil must really delight in getting someone to take up that course."[3] The devil will pull every trick he can to keep the people of God from spiritual warfare.

Be not in sin or defiled (unclean).

We must walk with kingdom principles. In other words, do not straddle the fence. When we straddle the fence, we are attempting to serve two masters. Jesus states, "No man can serve two masters: for either he will hate the one, and love the other; or else he will hold to the one, and despise the other. Ye cannot serve God and mammon" (Matt. 6:24).

You want to go into a deliverances session with clean hands, a clean heart, and humility. The only reason you have authority in the realm of darkness is because God has imparted it to you through the Holy Spirit in His Son's name (Jesus Christ).

Defiled or unclean could mean to be living a sinful life. It is possible you, yourself, are a carrier of an evil spirit. Remember Acts 19 when Paul was used by God to bring about special miracles? He released an anointing on handkerchiefs and aprons for the sick, and the diseases departed from them. The demons also went out of them.

Then certain of the vagabond Jews, exorcists, took upon them to call over them which had evil spirits the name of the LORD Jesus, saying, We adjure you by Jesus whom Paul preacheth. And there were seven sons of one Sceva, a Jew, and chief of the priests, which did so. And the evil spirit answered and said, Jesus I know, and Paul I know; but who are ye? And the man in whom the evil spirit was leaped on them, overcame them, and prevailed against them, so that they fled out of that house naked and wounded.

—ACTS 19:13–16

We see that dealing with demons is very serious work for the kingdom of God. Also deliverance is nothing to play with. Paul had a strong anointing on his life where not only sickness and diseases left a person but also evil spirits departed. In the Scripture these people (self-appointed) tried to free a possessed man and were whipped until they were naked. I do not know whether they were in sin or defiled (unclean) or not; but one thing is very clear, they did not have authority over demons. Therefore, be led by the Spirit. Do not go demon hunting. Only operate in deliverance when there is a need, the person wants to be set free, and the Spirit leads.

Let repentance be your lifestyle.

If my people, which are called by my name, shall humble themselves, and pray, and seek my face, and turn from their wicked ways; then will I

hear from heaven and will forgive their sins and
will heal their land.

—2 CHRONICLES 7:14

Repentance and living undefiled go hand in hand.
The only way you will live an undefiled life is to live a
life of repentance. When you sway to the left, repentance is necessary to walk in righteousness with the
Father (God). If you err, repent very soon. Do not wait
or postpone it. If you have pride, repent and ask God
to teach you by the Holy Spirit to walk in humility. If
pride is deeply rooted, bind and loose it from yourself
and cast it out. Remember, you can cast demons out
of your body and your soul yourself. As a deliverance
minister, you must stay prepared to minister deliverance to the captives. As a believer (not a deliverance
minister), you must also stay prepared to set the captives free.

Walk in the gift of faith.

There is another gift that is important during deliverance, and it is the gift of faith. During Daniel's
encounter in the lion's den, he did not believe from
natural faith. Natural faith is faith that comes from
hearing the word of God (Rom. 10:17). For example,
Elijah was fed by ravens in 1 Kings 17:3–6. "Elijah's
faith had to be given to him supernaturally because it
was beyond ordinary faith to believe that ravens would
feed him. But they brought food to him morning and
night….The gift of faith is employed in casting out evil
spirits. When you cast out devils, you are trusting God

to honor your word as his own....The gift of faith can expel unclean spirits from the bodies of men, which have been defiled by their presence."[4]

I urge you not to attempt a deliverance session if you are not living *completely* for God. Neither should you work with a team member who is walking in sin. It is very dangerous to do that; it could put you and the team member in a situation whereby the evil spirits leaving the person being worked on would transfer to the delivering minister. You must remain pure. (See 2 Chronicles 7:14.)

We should not just use lip service, but from the heart ask God to forgive us. We should ask each other for forgiveness—again from the heart. Forgiveness is a key to an area of deliverance. Ministers should not attempt deliverance with any uncleanness about themselves, not just unforgiveness. According to Basil Frasure, "We should daily yield our lives unto the Lord. We should walk in righteousness and holiness."[5] Yes, we should repent as needed.

I pray it has been made clear in other parts of this book that we as deliverance ministers need to have clean hands and a pure heart.

MY CALL TO DELIVERANCE MINISTRY

In 2001 I made a trip to a conference in Chicago, Illinois, with a couple of local women pastors. There were a couple of other people who also went with us to the conference. After one of the sessions, we all went out to eat lunch together. One of the pastors asked us what we were learning from the conference. Comments from the other members of the group were received positively. However, it seemed as though my answer was not good enough or was not the expected reply. I thought the conference was very good. I really learned and gained a lot from it. Kim Daniels was one of the keynote speakers. She was and remains strong in deliverance. She is also an apostle, and it seemed as though she really stirred up the demons. She did not do any casting out that night, but her message was powerful.

The next day we headed back to Omaha, praying and singing on the way. We played Kim Daniels' demon-buster tape. One of the women pastors began to get more and more anxious. We stopped by the other woman pastor's church because she was going to record some of the conference tapes they had told us we could duplicate. The pastor who felt anxious earlier began to talk about another pastor and how this person was a witch and another congregation member who she also called a witch. She said her husband was very close to the "witch" pastor. She said the pastor had given her some items for her house but she wanted to destroy them because she suspected they would open a door whereby evil could enter her home. Her husband was out of town.

When we arrived at her house, she suggested that we go in with her to destroy the items the pastor had given her. I said, "I don't believe your husband would like that. He would be very upset." While she continued to talk about the member who she accused of being a witch, the thought kept coming to me to tell her, "You are the witch." At that time I didn't realize that this thought was not my thought but it was coming from the evil influences of unclean spirits that were in the van.

After I told her that her husband would be upset if the items were destroyed, she told the driver to "back up, back up. Let's go." I told the driver to take me to my daughter's house where I had left my car. When we arrived I got out of the vehicle to get my luggage and the pastor got out also. The other two women got out as well to assist me.

A car drove past the driveway and the pastor began to point saying, "Who is that? Who is that?" I looked and told her I didn't know. I thought she was tired and needed to rest, so I hugged her and went on to say, "Get some rest," when full manifestation came forth. There were so many unclean spirits present—even from her childhood. The deliverance began at approximately 9:00 p.m. and ended about 5:00 a.m. Demons will try to hide from you.

At one point I said to her, "Let me hear your prayer language." When she proceeded, I realized that she still had not been set free because the prayer language was not her own. I would have recognized her prayer language, but this language I did not recognize. There was a lot of roaring and movement on the ground. The spirit of rejection, accuser of the brethren, and many spirits were commanded to come out in the name of Jesus; and they obeyed. Even though I was caught off guard, fear did not surface. As soon as I heard the roaring and smelled the foul odor, I knew demons had manifested. I began to say, "In the name of Jesus Christ, you come out of her." She began to break her necklace from her neck and fell to the ground. She not only began to break her necklace but also began to writhe on the ground like a snake. I cast out the spirit of murder, the spirit of rejection, the spirit of perversion, and other demons as they were identified. At one point she called me by name, saying, "Loreatha, help me." I told her she was almost free. She said, "I wear so many faces, half the time I don't even know who I am."

I looked around for the two young women who had gotten out of the car to help me with my luggage. They had jumped into the car. The car door was open, and in the light I could see they were huddled up together in fetal positions. I called out to them to go and get another pastor. They were glad to go. The other pastor came and we both worked with getting the troubled pastor set free.

God had chosen me to be the leading deliverance minister because this was to be the beginning of a new level for me. This was the fulfillment of the prophecy given to me at the Grand Island conference.

During this deliverance I was screaming and yelling,

"In the name of Jesus, come out; I plead the blood of Jesus; shut up and come out of her." I don't know why someone did not call the police because I was so loud. I don't remember the pastor who was assisting screaming her commands. Later on God told me, "You do not have to do all of that; just speak softly with authority and the demons will obey you, for I have given you authority." I was so happy God told me that because I was hoarse for about three weeks afterwards. After that deliverance God began to use me often to set people free.

I cannot stress enough that you should *know* you have the authority and walk in the gift of faith. God performed special miracles through apostle Paul. Paul had such great faith and anointing on his life that from his body the sick were healed from aprons or handkerchiefs, and disease left the people along with evil spirits (Acts 19:12).

> Then certain of the vagabond Jews, exorcists, took upon them to call over them which had evil spirits the name of the LORD Jesus, saying, We adjure you by Jesus whom Paul preacheth. And there were seven sons of one Sceva, a Jew, and chief of the priests, which did so. And the evil spirit answered and said, Jesus I know, and Paul I know; but who are ye? And the man in whom the evil spirit was leaped on them, overcame them, and prevailed against them, so that they fled out of that house naked and wounded.
>
> —ACTS 19:13–16

From this scripture you can see why it is important that you have authority to set free those who are being held in bondage by Beelzebub. We have authority; but it is one thing to have authority and another to *know* you have authority. Mark 16:17a states: "And these signs shall follow them that believe; in my name shall they cast out devils." Walk with holy boldness! You can do the same thing Jesus did and more because He went to sit at the right side of his Father (God) (John 14:12). You can be an apostle, a prophet or prophetess, an evangelist, a pastor, a teacher, or a lay person.

A theological degree is not required but one does need to understand that "deliverance ministry is biblically sound, know their spiritual authority in Jesus Christ, are empowered with the Gift of the Holy Spirit, have compassion for the oppressed, carry a special love for children, and are willing to step out in faith and are not afraid of making mistakes."[6]

I want to emphasize that you should not work alone. Always work with at least one more person. If the minister is female and the person being delivered is male, then have a male as your helper. However, you can bring in another female to intercede. Both the male and female can be praying while the minister is binding and casting out the demons in the name of Jesus. As the Holy Spirit reveals the realm of darkness to the team, it should be shared with the head minister. The head minister should never go into a deliverance session thinking he or she will be the only one who will discern what evil spirits the individual is a carrier of, especially if they have received any of the three gifts we used as recognizing demons: gift of wisdom, gift of the word of knowledge, and the discerning of spirits.

After the deliverance session ends, always pray over and with the person and release an anointing upon them. Also, release an impartation or transference of the anointing of the Holy Spirit to the individual. Emotional healing should take place after deliverance. You should always fill the area where evil spirits were nesting with the anointing. Become a deliverance minister who is led by the Spirit of God.

CHAPTER 5

STAYING FREE OF DEMONS

POSTLE PAUL, WHO wrote two-thirds of the New Testament, has a solution for remaining free from demons. In Ephesians 6 he states the following:

> Finally, my brethren, be strong in the Lord, and in the power of his might. Put on the whole armour of God, that ye may be able to stand against the wiles of the devil. For we wrestle not against principalities, against powers, against the rulers of darkness of this world, against spiritual wickedness in high places.
>
> —EPHESIANS 6:10–12

Methodeias (Greek) means methods—the different means, plans, and schemes used to deceive, entrap, enslave, and ruin the souls of men. A man's method of sinning is the devil's method of damning his soul.

Paul's instructions in verses 10 through 12 were to put on the whole armor of God. In verses 13–18 he continues with these commands:

> Wherefore take unto you the whole armour of God, that ye may be able to withstand in the evil day, and having done all, to stand. Stand therefore, having your loins girt about with truth, and having on the breastplate of righteousness; And your feet shod with the preparation of the gospel of peace; Above all, taking the shield of faith, wherewith ye shall be able to quench all the fiery darts of the wicked. And take the helmet of salvation and the sword of the Spirit, which is the word of God: Praying always with all prayer and supplication in the Spirit, and watching thereunto with all perseverance and supplication for all saints.
>
> —EPHESIANS 6:13–18

According to *Dake's Annotated Reference Bible,* Paul says, "Having laid before you your high calling and the great doctrine of the Gospel, I will now show you the enemies that will oppose you and how you can overcome them."[1]

Twelve Commands for Saints:

Be strong in the Lord;

Be strong in His power;

Put on the whole armor of God;

Stand;

Have your loins girt with truth;

Put on the breastplate of righteousness;

Have your feet shod with the preparation of the
gospel of peace;

Take the shield of faith;

Take the helmet of salvation;

Take the sword of the Spirit;

Pray in the Spirit; and

Watch in prayer.

We can remain free if we follow Paul's blueprint.
Be strong in the Lord by not allowing the devil to
come to us with lies. He is the father of lies (John
8:44). He may otherwise cause us to get weak towards
God with negative thoughts. This will give him a legal
right to oppress, depress, or enter our souls. If we put
on the whole armor of God and walk in every part of
it, we can and will remain free of demons activity in
our bodies, soul, and lives.

The armor reveals we should take up the shield of
faith, because with faith men shall be able to quench
all the fiery darts of the wicked. Dake identifies four
spirit rebels:

> Gr *Archas*—Principalities, chief rulers or being
> of the highest rank and order in Satan's kingdom
> (v. 12; 1:21; Colossians 2:10)
> Gr. *Exousias*—Authorities. Those who drive
> their power from and execute the will of the
> chief rulers. (v 12; 1:21; Col. 2:10)
> Gr. *Komokratopas*—World rulers of the

darkness of this age, the spirit world- rulers (Dan. 10:13–21; Eph. 1:21; 6:12; Col 1:16–18)

Gr. *Pneumatika ponerias*—Spiritual wicked-ness, that of the wicked spirits of Satan in the heavenlies (v 12: 1:21; Col. 1:16–18)

The above Greek names of Spirits are those high-ranking demons of the principalities. These demons are like the army's ranking starting with the very highest ranks.[2]

Then we have the fiery darts:

Gr. *Belos*—Dart, or any missile thrown as the javelin, spear, arrow, or stone from a sling. The fiery darts perhaps refer to the combustible arrowheads that set fire to the fortifications, ships, houses, and even the shields of the enemy made of wood and leather. They were called *fal-orica*. To quench these fiery darts, shields were covered with metal. As applied to Christian warfare, they refer to evil thoughts, lust, pas-sions, and temptations of various kinds. (1 Cor. 10:13–14; 2 Cor. 10:4–6; Jas. 1:13–15; Rom. 6:12; 1 John 2:15–17)[3]

Therefore, the fiery darts are things where Christians can fall into the traps of Satan. Lust can cause a door to be open for Satan to have a legal right to enter us. We can lust after many things. Lust is a deep craving for a person, place, or thing. It can be someone else's spouse (adultery). One can crave drugs or gambling if he or she falls into temptation, as our first mother,

Eve, did. The door once again is open to Satan and his demons.

After falling prey to the enemy a few times, the Holy Spirit has taught me how to remain free of spirits entering my soul. In addition to keep demons from entering my body and oppressing me from the outside of my being, I have learned to remain strong in my salvation. I pray daily and read the word of God and I praise and worship God daily. I protect my eye and ear gates. That means I pay attention to what movies or television programs I watch. My spirit only enjoys gospel music. Every so often I go through my house and cleanse it of anything that's not like God. When you have different people in and out of your house, it needs to be anointed and demonic spirits need to be commanded to leave the house and premises. Many times after a deliverance session, I will make a deliverance call on myself. When I do that, it is to make sure nothing is in my soul or that nothing has followed me home to set up residence.

Always go into your prayer closet and demand all unclean spirits to leave you, your family, and your household.

> Search me, O God, and know my heart: try me, and know my thoughts: And see if there be any wicked way in me, and lead me in the way everlasting.
> —PSALM 139:23–24

Another thing, you must commit to God 100 percent not 99 percent. You cannot play with sin if you want to stay free. Iron sharpens iron (Prov. 27:17). In other words, associate with people who are really seeking God and you know for a fact they love Jesus and are followers of the Holy Spirit. Be careful where you go. Only go to churches where the presence of God is moving and the Word of God is being taught and presented. Also watch what you speak. Always speak the Word of God. If you are a deliverance minister, ask people of prayer to always "cover" you. Also as a minister you must pray without ceasing and meditate on the word of God. Worshipping God is very necessary. Worship as often as you can. Don't depend on others to cover you. Keep yourself covered with the blood of Jesus. Also keep your entire family covered with the blood of Jesus and claim a hedge for you and then your family.

Spiritual cleansing of your home is very important. If you are married, many times arguments start over very small issues. If you are single, you may hear unexplained noises. While you are asleep sexual demons may attempt to penetrate if you are a female, or try homosexual acts on a male if he is single.

Apostle Ivory L. Hopkins in his *Spiritual Warfare Training Manual* describes the sexual demons as incubus, who have sexual intercourse with women, and succubus, who attack men. He gives the following examples and explanations:

A lady called me on the phone one evening and said, "I'm the bride of Christ (Revelation 21:9–10) and Jesus has been visiting me." Later, she said, "He has been taking care of my sexual needs; I don't need a man." Days later, she calls me and says that Jesus is having physical sex with her. I knew that she was being attacked by an incubus spirit counterfeiting Jesus. We took authority over the spirit that was sexually attacking her and command it to leave and God set her free. (Note: her family had been known to practice witchcraft in gambling and other areas of their lives. Thank God many have repented and become Christians). *Incubus* is defined as 1) an evil spirit believed to descend upon and have sexual intercourse with women as they sleep. 2) A nightmare. 3) An oppressive or nightmarish burden. In this lady's case, the spirit started penetrating her body sexually, causing extreme pain. This type of spirit will get on top of a person and cause them to feel as if they are suffocating. It can somehow operate in the dream realm, with sexual attacks.

Please excuse my bluntness, but there is a difference in this type of sexual dream and what we call a "wet dream." Wet dreams come from a build up of semen and are not demonic manifestations. A wet dream is an erotic dream accompanied by ejaculation of semen. When it is a demonic manifestation of Incubus (attacks women) or Succubus (attacks men), the victim feels under siege and, in most cases, can feel a physical presence on top of them. I heard of a preacher that told a lady in this church he would take care of her sexual needs and not have sex with her in person but that he would come in the spirit at night and take care of her sexual needs. Sure enough, at night a spirit that looked just like him would come and have sex with her. I had her to renounce the acceptances of these types of manifestations and to command the familiar spirit of the preacher to leave in Jesus name. Now, she no longer has these types of sexual, demonic attacks.[4]

As a deliverance minister, I have been called in to spiritually cleanse many houses. I usually interview the owners of the home. Most of the time it is the wife with whom I speak. As I interviewed the wife and mother of two children, she explained the daughter was not able to sleep at night. She would always go and get in the bed with mom and dad.

I started upstairs anointing the doorpost in every room along with the front and back door. I pled the blood of Jesus over each doorpost as I anointed them with olive oil (symbolic of the Holy Spirit). I went downstairs and followed the same process. All of a sudden we heard the sound of a door closing very loudly. We (the mother and me) looked at each other and exclaimed, "Wow!" The daughter never had another sleepless night. Many times I am called in to bless the home when a family moves into a new house or apartment. I often go through my own home and cleanse it—again using the same process mentioned above.

Last summer I learned an extension to the process

of cleaning a house and property. I am a member of a team chosen by God to pray for the City of Omaha. We had a Healing the Land team that came into our city from the island of Fiji. We were taught how to cleanse houses and defiled sites. Now when I am called in to cleanse a house, I also cleanse the property of evil spirits. I not only anoint the doorposts and pray but also use the following process: (1) Mix olive oil with salt and water, (2) interview the family, (3) anoint every family member, (4) anoint each doorpost, (5) go from room to room anointing the furniture and sprinkling the mixture onto every area of the dwelling, (6) and go outside and sprinkle the mixture over the entire property.

The anointing elements are applied to everyone and everything in the house. I do not service a home alone. While I am interviewing the family, an intercessor is standing in the gap for me and the family. There are usually three of us serving the household with deliverance. I call it a type of deliverance, because often family members get set free of evil spirits. Demons are commanded to leave the family's home.

A lot of time the family members are delivered when asked about their childhood. We would reveal molestation with the operation of discerning of spirits. On one occasion it was revealed the father had unforgiveness for his son. The father felt like the son was keeping his grandchildren from him and the grandmother. He stated, "He never comes home." Of course we shared the Word of God on forgiveness and he forgave his son. The spirit of unforgiveness left through the Word of God. Before we left the family, we released the anointing of the Holy Spirit upon them and in the home.

One home we went to, the father was a widower. His wife had passed away many years before. He was the father of five children. Only two of them were present for the deliverance. There was a lot of unforgiveness in the heart of the oldest daughter. She accused the father of allowing a member of the church to chase her and her husband away from the church. She called the member a Jezebel. The Jezebel spirit describes anyone who acts in the same manner as Jezebel did—engaging in immorality, idolatry, false teaching, and unrepentant sin. Where there is a Jezebel Spirit, there is an Ahab Spirit. The Jezebel spirit is one that manipulates others, especially the pastor and other leaders of a church. She has to be in control of things. She has to have her way with things. When the pastor and leaders wake up, they have no authority. Jezebel is in full control. She is rebellion's (witchcraft) twin.

During the session, the daughter forgave her father but not the member she had named Jezebel. The property was cleansed and the anointing of the Holy Spirit was released in the home and upon the property. The Holy Spirit is a deliverer for God's people.

CHAPTER 6

HIERARCHY OF SATANIC SPIRITS AND THEIR ASSIGNMENTS

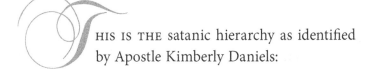HIS IS THE satanic hierarchy as identified by Apostle Kimberly Daniels:

- Satan—the prince of the power of the air

- Beelzebub—the prince of the devils; answers directly and only to Satan

- Principalities—princes of the four corners of the earth: continents, countries, states, cities, counties (*arche*—magistrate or principle demons, first in rank)

- Powers—organizations (*exousia*—special ability; highly competent; liberty in jurisdiction); ruler spirits: neighborhoods, families, individuals (*kosmokrator*—world ruler; spirits with direct contact with its target)

- Spiritual wickedness in high places—idolatry (Hezekiah tore down the high places) (*poneria*—inquity and malice; sin and idolatrous activity)

- Generational princes of devils—during the era of the Philistines, Dagon; during the era of Elijah, Baal; during the era of Jesus, Beelzebub. (The goal of demonic authority in "territorial" warfare is displacement to remove all opposition and to occupy in authority.)[1]

The satanic hierarchy shows how the demons are ranked. Satan is the head. He has many demons to which he gives assignments. As a baby grows up to become an adult, we as spiritual babies grow up to become spiritually mature. As we mature, the devil assigns different demons to us at different levels. He knows our purpose and destiny better than we do. I believe when we come to the age of accountability, he sends some pretty strong demons to attack us. A lot of us call the age of accountability twelve years old because that's the age Jesus went to the temple and spoke with the elders with wisdom (Luke 2:42–47).

Everyone does not mature at the same age in the natural nor the spiritual. At each level of maturity, I believe Satan sends his most powerful demon for you. In other words, he will send the one who can steal your focus, the one who will attack you in order for you to fall into sin. Demons are assigned to you to follow you around and spy on you. They will whisper different thoughts in your ear, and you will accept them as your own.

SATAN

Satan is the prince of the power of the air, the abode of the prince of the air; positioned between the first and third heavens. In 2 Corinthians 10:5 it speaks of "casting down...every high thing [Greek *hypsoma*] that exalteth itself against the knowledge of God and bringing into captivity every thought to the obedience of Christ." That's why Michael and the angels kicked Satan and one third of the angels led by him out of the third heaven. Now Satan lives or hangs out in the second heaven.

In answer to the question, "What is heaven like?" Got Questions Ministries in Colorado responded as follows:

> Heaven is a real place described in the Bible. The word "heaven" is found 276 times in the New Testament alone. Scripture refers to three heavens. The first is most frequently referred to in the Old Testament as the "sky" or the "firmament," which appears as an arch that is spread over our earth. This is the heaven that contains clouds, the area that birds fly through. The

second heaven is the interstellar space, which is the abode of supernatural angelic beings and celestial objects (Genesis 1:14–18). The third heaven, whose location is unrevealed, is the abode of the Triune God. God's plan is to fill heaven with believers in Jesus Christ. No wonder the word heaven is interchangeable with eternal life! Jesus promised to prepare a place for true Christians in heaven (John 14:2). The Apostle Paul was "caught up to the third heaven," but he was prohibited from revealing what he experienced there (2 Corinthians 12:1–9).[2]

BEELZEBUB

Beelzebub is called "the prince of the devils" in Matthew 12:24. Matthew 10:25b tells us, "If they have called the master of the house Beelzebub, how much more shall they call them of his household?

According to Dake's Bible, "In the Greek, it is Beelzebub, lord of abominable idols; the prince of idols and idolatry; the worst prince of idols and idolatry; the worst and chief of all wickedness. To inquire of such a god was to deny Jehovah."[3]

> And Ahaziah fell down through a lattice in his upper chamber that was in Samaria, and was sick: and he sent messengers, and said unto them, Go enquire of Baalzebub the god of Ekron whether I shall recover of this disease.
> —2 KINGS 1:2

He did not ask the true and living God if he would live. Beelzebub was the god of flies. later the Jews changed the name to Beelzebub dunghill god. He was identified as prince of demons.

PRINCIPALITIES

Princes of the four corners of the earth cover continents, countries, states, cities, counties. Satan is the prince and ruler of the air (second heaven). He dwells in the realm of darkness with dominion over all demons (*arche*—magistrate or first in rank).

POWERS

Exousia means special ability, highly competent, liberty in jurisdiction.[4] Satan does have special ability, however, it is not greater than God's people and yes, he is competent in many areas. But he is not more competent than God. God tells us to strive to have the mind of Christ. He does have a lot of liberty in jurisdiction. That's because the Saints of God allow it. The Bible tells us to resist the devil and he will flee from us. Satan has got no more power than we allow him to have. For greater is he who is on the inside of us than he who is in the world.

Kosmokrator means world ruler; spirits with direct contact with its target.[5] Ruler spirits are those by which neighborhoods, families and individuals are tormented. Ruler spirits rule over certain areas with other lower ranking demons. I strongly believe that in

Omaha the ruler spirits are pride and murder. The targets are leaders and very young people (our future).

SPIRITUAL WICKEDNESS IN HIGH PLACES

Spiritual wickedness in high places manifests itself in idolatry or iniquity and malice and sin and idolatrous activity.[6]

> But if ye say unto me, We trust in the LORD our God: is not that he, whose high places and whose altars Hezekiah hath taken away, and hath said to Judah and Jerusalem, ye shall worship before this altar in Jerusalem?
>
> —2 KINGS 18:22

This shows ignorance of the Assyrians concerning Hezekiah's actions. Hezekiah had taken all the high places of Baal away and removed all Baal's worship. The Assyrians thought Hezekiah had removed Jehovah's worship places, but that was not the case.

Poneria is another word for iniquity and malice, sin and idolatrous activity.[7]

GENERATIONAL PRINCE OF DEVILS

These demons can be curses that come down through the bloodline—high blood pressure, diabetes, cancer, alcoholic addiction and many other diseases. These all may be generational curses brought on by unclean spirits.

THE STRONGMAN AND OTHER SPIRITS

Strongman

Jesus was accused of casting out demons by the power of the devil.

> And if I by Beelzebub cast out devils, by whom do your children cast them out? therefore, they shall be your judges. But if I cast out devils by the Spirit of God, then the kingdom of God is come unto you. Or else how can one enter into a strong man's house, and spoil his goods, except he first bind the strong man? Then he will spoil his house.
>
> —MATTHEW 12:27–29

There may be a grouping of spirits in the soul or body. You can be assured there is a strongman—a demon that is stronger than the rest of the evil spirits. Often if you identify the strongman, there is no problem casting out the other spirits. The following unclean spirits are strongman spirits followed by weaker spirits.

Spirit of infirmity

"And, behold, there was a woman which had a spirit of infirmity eighteen years, and was bowed together, and could in no wise lift up herself" (Luke 13:11).

Some other examples of the spirit of infirmity:

- Man could not walk for thirty-eight years (John 5:5)

- Sinus problems

- Bloody flux (Acts 28:8)

- Arthritis (crippling of the joints)

- Gout (inflammation in joints)

Remember you can free yourself from the devil. "Submit yourselves therefore to God. Resist the devil, and he will flee from you" (James 4:7).

Spirit of jealousy

"And the spirit of jealousy came upon him, and he be jealous of his wife, and she be defiled: or if the spirit of jealousy come upon him, and he be jealous of his wife, and she be not defiled: Then shall the man bring his wife unto the priest" (Num. 5:14–15). Cain killed Abel because of his jealousy of Abel's relationship with God (Gen. 4:8).

Manifestations of the spirit of jealousy:

- Envy of another person

- Selfishness

- Hate

- Spite

- Anger

- Suspiciousness

- Coveting

- Competition

- Rage

- Suicide

- Murder

- Injury to another (hurt)

Spirit of divination

> And it came to pass, as we went to prayer, a certain damsel possessed with a spirit of divination met us, which brought her masters much gain by soothsaying: The same followed Paul and us, and cried, saying, These men are the servants of the most high God, which shew unto us the way of salvation. And this she did many days. But Paul, being grieved, turned and said to the spirit, I command thee in the name of Jesus Christ to come out of her. And he came out the same hour.
> —Acts 16:16–18

Paul's spirit was grieved. I suggest it was the Holy Spirit who was grieved and revealed to Paul the unclean spirit. Every word the girl spoke seems true, but Satan's plan was to discredit Paul's message by making the people believe they were involved with demon spirits. The young woman was a possessed medium. The devil wanted the people to think the apostles were doing miracles by the devil and not God. Paul saw the purpose of Satan; so he turned to the demon, not the girl, and cast out the spirit of divination.

Spirit of flattery and spirit of control

I understand these two spirits work hand-in-hand.

Spirit of flattery

"Flattery defined: Insincere praise or compliments of personal interest or motives."[8]

> They speak vanity everyone with his neighbour: with flattering lips and with a double heart do they speak. The LORD shall cut off all flattering lips, and the tongue that speaketh proud things.
> —PSALM 12:2–3

Also,

> A man that flattereth his neighbor spreadeth a net for his feet.
> —PROVERBS 29:5

Pastor Hopkins tells us to "watch for such statements as, 'You're such an understanding pastor,' or, 'You're so mightily used of the Lord and so gifted.' One thing that a pastor or church leader must understand is that you are in a position that there is little praise or encouragement; so don't flatter so easily."[9]

He further states that "the hurts and rejections of the ministry can open you up to being prey to spirits of control through flattery; then they will drop you like a hot potato when they are finished with you. There are those in the body of Christ who are sincere about what they say to you, but always keep in mind to try the spirits whether they be of God. Don't live off of compliments, but live to obey the will of God, whether you are praised by men or not."[10]

In this regard he refers to the following scriptures: "Woe unto you, when all men shall speak well of you! for so did their fathers to the false prophets" (Luke 6:26). Also, "Now when he was in Jerusalem at the passover, on the feast day, many believed in his name, when they saw the miracles which he did. But Jesus did not commit himself unto them, because he knew all men, And needed not that any should testify of man: for he knew what was in man" (John 2:23–25).

Another spirit that works along with the spirit of flattery is the spirit of control. Be wary of a person who is a carrier of a spirit of control.

Spirit of control

Pastor Hopkins says that "Control Spirits in a person will claim to be under headship of a pastor while not really submitting to anyone. As long as the pastor does what they want, he's their pastor, but woe unto you if you fall out of their grace....All control spirits must have the center of the stage. Those who have control spirits, if they are not leading things, they do not feel, 'so-called' led to be a part of what's going on."[11]

Control spirits have many attributes. They want to

control every single aspect of your life, changing you into what they have decided you need to be. Pastor Hopkins refers to 2 Timothy 2:15, "Study to shew thyself approved unto God, a workman that needeth not be ashamed, rightly dividing the word of truth." He explains that "this means that each believer is to study for themselves; not to get all the revelations of God from someone else, and don't be amazed at any man or woman, just Jesus."[12]

Leviathan—the king of pride

Leviathan is talked about in the following scriptures: Job 41:1–34, Isaiah 27:1, and Revelation 12. In Job 41:34 it says, "He beholdeth all high things: he is the king over all the children of pride." Isaiah 27:1 tells us, "In that day the LORD with his sore and great and strong sword shall punish leviathan the piercing serpent, even leviathan that crooked serpent; and he shall slay the dragon that is in the sea." And in Revelation 12 we read:

> And there was war in heaven: Michael and his angels fought against the dragon; and the dragon fought and his angels, And prevailed not; neither was their place found anymore in heaven. And the great dragon was cast out, that old serpent, called the devil, and Satan, which deceiveth the whole world: he was cast out into the earth, and his angels were cast out with him.
>
> —REVELATION 12:7–9

Some Christians consider Leviathan to be a demon associated with Satan or the devil:

> Awake, awake, put on strength, O arm of the Lord: awake, as in the ancient days, in the generations of old. Art thou not it that hath cut Rahab, and wounded the dragon?
>
> —Isaiah 51:9

> Thou didst divide the sea by the strength: thou breaketh the heads of the dragons in the waters. Thou breakest the heads of leviathan in pieces, and gavest him to be meat to the people inhabiting the wilderness.
>
> —Psalm 74:13–14

Leviathan is symbolic of pride. Leviathan is a tough dinosaur. The Bible describes it as being hard to handle. There is no hook that will be able to catch him. That's the way pride works. It is hard to get rid of. In 2 Kings 18:22 the manifestation is the twins: rebellion and witchcraft. Then you have self-exaltation and haughtiness. Pride is very hard to deal with. Most people will swear they do not have pride. Therefore, Satan is having a field day in some families and in our places of worship. Satan has people thinking they are a certain denomination, and it becomes a point of pride. People will think they have crossed over to that denomination if they associate with people of a particular domination. Not only is this pride but it brings about division in the body of Christ.

Spirit of haughtiness

"Pride goeth before destruction, and an haughty spirit before a fall. Better it is to be of an humble spirit with the lowly, than to divide the spoil with the proud" (Prov. 16:18–19).

The spirit of haughtiness is manifested through:

- Lofty looks

- Egotism

- Rigidity

- Boastfulness

- Pride

> These six things doeth the LORD hate: yea, seven are an abomination unto him: A proud look, a lying tongue, and hands that shed innocent blood, An heart that deviseth wicked imaginations, feet that be swift in running to mischief, A false witness that speaketh lies, and he that soweth discord among brethren.
>
> —PROVERBS 6:16–19

Perverse spirit

"The LORD hath mingled a perverse spirit in the midst thereof: and they have caused Egypt to err in every work thereof, as a drunken man staggereth in his vomit?" (Isa. 19:14). Manifestations of perverse spirits:

- Homosexuality

- Prostitution

- Oral sex

- Masturbation

- Self lovers: "This know also, that in the last days perilous times shall come. For men shall be lovers of their own selves, covetous, boasters, proud, blasphemers, disobedient to parents, unthankful, unholy" (2 Tim. 3:1–2).

- Lust: "Thine eyes shall behold strange women, and thine heart shall utter perverse things" (Prov. 23:33). "Teaching us that, denying ungodliness and worldly lusts, we should live soberly, righteously, and godly, in this present world" (Titus 2:12).

Spirit of heaviness

"To appoint unto them that mourn in Zion, to give unto them beauty for ashes, the oil of joy for mourning, the garment of praise for the spirit of heaviness; that they might be called trees of righteousness, the planting of the LORD, that he might be glorified" (Isa. 61:3).

Manifestations of this spirit are:

- Grief

- Despair

- Loneliness

- Rejection

- Self-pity (Ps. 69:20)

- Depression

- Oppression

Spirit of fear

"For God hath not given us the spirit of fear; but of power, and of love, and of a sound mind" (2 Tim. 1:7). Manifestations of the spirit of fear are:

- Fear

- Torment: "There is no fear in love; but perfect love casteth out fear: because fear hath torment. He that feareth is not made perfect in love" (1 John 4:18).

- Nightmares

- Inferiority

- Stress

- Schizophrenia

Perfect love indeed casteth out all fear. As we continue our discourse, you will discover how the Holy Spirit can lead us from the darkness of demonic possessions into the Father's (God's) marvelous light.

CHAPTER 7
HOLY SPIRIT: THE DELIVERER

*M*Y EXPLANATION OF the Holy Spirit is that He has a personality, can grieve, and can be quenched. Who is this Holy Spirit? This Spirit is the third person of the Godhead: God the Father, God the son, and God the Holy Spirit. During Israel's mission God told them,

> Ye are my witnesses, saith the LORD, and my servant whom I have chosen: that ye may know and believe me, and understand that I am he; before me there was no God formed, neither shall there be after me. I, even I, am the LORD; and beside me there is no saviour.
>
> —ISAIAH 43:10–11

God let the people of Israel know that He has always been and before Him there was no one. Then you have Jesus who was with God from the beginning. When time came, He came in the flesh (God in the flesh). He gave His life for all mankind. He gave it so we can not only have eternal life but to show us we can have an abundant life on earth. "I am come that they might have life, and that they might have it more abundantly" (John 10:10b). He came to set the captives free and mend the brokenhearted. Jesus, as He was leaving the earth, prayed to the Father to send another comforter (God the Holy Spirit), who came fifty days after Christ was crucified (John 14:16; Acts 2:1-4).

So, really, who is the Holy Spirit and what are His attributes on earth? We are going to look at other documentation, but I want to first share my insight and revelation of His actions and why Jesus prayed to the Father to send Him to the earth. Don't forget, Jesus went and sat at the right hand side of God the Father after He prayed that the Holy Spirit would come and dwell in the earth as the new comforter to God's people (Mark 15:19; Acts 2:33). The Father answered Jesus' prayer and the Holy Spirit arrived in His fullness on the Day of Pentecost. His attributes began that day as Peter, the spokesman for the apostles, went forth and preached a sermon, leading about three thousand people to conversion (Acts 2:41). The first congregation (church) was established through the Holy Spirit.

The New Testament provides a very good picture of how the first church looked and carried out its ministry. We should all agree that the Holy Spirit is the one who enables us to perform any work that pleases the Father (John 15:5; Acts 1:8). Therefore, what you see in the New Testament is how the Spirit chooses to work through the church.

I have written about who the Holy Spirit is, but I would like to go deeper and talk about what the Holy Spirit does. I don't claim to know everything He does; however, I believe I have had a revelation of an area where the Holy Spirit operates that is not recognized by some people. Many of us do not have a practical understanding of the Holy Spirit. Many have not heard of the Holy Spirit. There are a few who have heard of Him but do not understand His role as the third person of the Godhead. Some believe at conversion they have been filled with the Spirit of God. They are partially right, but not 100 percent. When we accept Jesus Christ as our personal Savior, the Spirit of God is who brings life to us. He, through our faith, gives birth to our dead spirit.

However, the baptism of the Holy Spirit is a separate gift from the gift of salvation. God gives us this promise: "If ye then, being evil, know how to give good gifts unto your children: how much more shall your heavenly Father give the Holy Spirit to them who ask him?" (Luke 11:13). There are others who believe the Holy Spirit is all about tongues. Of course, tongues are the evidence of the infilling of the Holy Spirit. There is much, much more to the Holy Spirit. I am not saying He will not speak to you if you are not filled, but He cannot use you like He can a person who has been filled and receives power from on high. Apostle Paul commanded all Christians to become filled with the

Holy Spirit: "And be not drunk with wine, wherein is excess; but be filled with the Spirit" (Eph. 5:18).

The Holy Spirit is omnipresent, meaning He is everywhere all the time. (See Psalm 139:7–12 and 1 Corinthians 2:10.) *Omniscient* means God knows all. We cannot hide anything from God. *Omnipotent* means all powerful. God is all powerful. He can do all things (Job 42:2).

"How God anointed Jesus of Nazareth with the Holy Ghost and with power: who went about doing good, and healing all that were oppressed of the devil; for God was with him" (Acts 10:38). As the Holy Spirit anointed Jesus by the hand of God, He will anoint you and He will anoint me with power.

The purpose of the baptism of the Holy Spirit as told in Acts 2:1–4, is to have power from on high (Luke 24:49). One does not have the fullness of the Holy Spirit until he or she has received the infilling of the Holy Spirit. We need the Holy Spirit. It is given to us for:

1. Witnessing power: Peter became a power-house for God. (See Acts 2:41.)

2. Working power: Spirit-filled Christians are able to carry out God's work (natural and supernatural). (See 1 Corinthians 12:4–11, 28.)

The work of the Holy Spirit can be found throughout the Old and New Testaments. I want you to examine the following scriptures for some of His works:

> But ye shall receive power, after that the Holy Ghost is come upon you: and ye shall be witnesses unto me both in Jerusalem, and in all Judea, and in Samaria, and unto the uttermost part of the earth.
>
> —ACTS 1:8

I want you to really focus on this scripture. Don't forget He is in us and He comes upon us. Therefore, we are ready and able to ambush the kingdom of darkness, not only setting others free but we too can become free of unclean spirits.

> The Holy Spirit wants to work in the hearts and lives of men and women. He can do more for us in a few moments than we can do for ourselves in our lifetime. He wants to fill us, empower us, and work through us.[1]

The Holy Spirit enables us to walk in the power of the gifts—the same spiritual gifts we shared in recognizing demons.

> Power to discern: spiritual gifts help us discern God's will and way. They also help us discern the nature of a problem as well as a way to solve that problem. Power to denounce and destroy: Spiritual gifts are backed by the power to denounce the powers of sin, sickness, Satan and his demons.[2]

> Verily, verily, I say unto you, He that believeth
> on me, the work that I do shall he do also; and
> greater works than these shall he do; because I
> go unto my Father.
>
> —JOHN 14:12

Jesus made this scriptural promise to every believer. As He walked the earth, He was localized because He was in the flesh and therefore not omnipresent. He was just as all other human beings. Jesus was limited on earth in knowledge and other powers. Please do not misunderstand me. Yes, He was God in the flesh. However, He said, "Greater works than these shall he do; because I go to the Father." I believe Jesus stated we can do greater things, not only because He was going to the Father but also because He prayed to the Father to send another Comforter (the Holy Spirit), who came the day of Pentecost.

Jesus says in Luke 10:19: "Behold I give unto you power [authority] to tread on serpents and scorpions, and over all the power of the enemy: and nothing by any means shall hurt you." We certainly must have authority; but we also need the Holy Spirit working through us and along with us, just as we do not speak in tongues on our own (the Holy Spirit gives the utterance). We are not delivering people on our own. The Holy Spirit is working through us as we make the command in the name of Jesus (come out of him or her).

Jesus also stated in John 14:14: "If ye ask anything in my name, I will do it." Jesus is speaking to people who believe in Him and are led by the Holy Spirit. Jesus was accused of casting demons out by Beelzebub in Luke 11:15. He told them in verse 20, "But if I with the finger of God cast out devils, no doubt the kingdom of God is come upon you." When Jesus speaks of the finger of God, He is using it figuratively. He is really saying He is casting demons out by the Spirit of God (the Holy Spirit). In Matthew 12:28, Jesus makes it very clear, "But if I cast out devils by the Spirit of God, then the kingdom of God is come unto you."

The Holy Spirit is the breath of God, and He carries the voice of God. That's why we must be careful of what we say. We must speak positive over our lives and our children, grandchildren, etc., because there is life and death in the power of the tongue (Prov. 18:21). Therefore, when we speak, it is God speaking when we are in the will of God. Casting out demons is the will of God.

I know I have authority in the realm of darkness. However, I never want to go into a deliverance session without the Holy Spirit walking in with me. Jesus gives us authority to cast out demons. The Holy Spirit is our power as we go forth in deliverance.

David states in Psalm 51, verse 11: "Cast me not away from thy presence; and take not thy Holy Spirit from me." It is important to live a committed life to God the Father. God will not dwell in an unclean temple (human being). First Samuel 10:9–13 shows how Saul was anointed as king and the Spirit of God came upon him. After Pentecost the Spirit was in us and can come upon us. In addition, during any kind of ministry, the Holy Spirit is present.

In the beginning God created the heaven and the earth and the earth was not yet formed. "And darkness was upon the face of the deep. And the Spirit of God moved upon the face of the waters" (Gen. 1:2). As the Holy Spirit hovered over the waters and the land, God spoke and created the earth and all that was within it (see Gen. 1).

"Likewise the Spirit also helpeth our infirmities: for we know not what we should pray for as we ought: but the Spirit itself maketh intercession for us with groanings which cannot be uttered" (Rom. 8:26). I contend the Holy Spirit is in us and with us during all ministry. I believe His presence is what keeps the minister from being attacked by demons that are being cast out.

Being filled with the Spirit of God or baptized in the Holy Spirit is a gift from God letting the Spirit control our lives to manifest Him during ministry of any kind. We are then filled with the Spirit of God and we will act like God, as did Paul and Peter. As mentioned earlier, to be possessed with an evil spirit causes you to act like that spirit. When Jesus walked the earth, He was full of the Spirit of God, acted like God, and was God. He cast out demons by the Spirit of God.

God used Paul to heal the sick and get rid of demons that vexed the people. "And God wrought special miracles by the hand of Paul. So that from his body were brought unto the sick handkerchiefs or aprons, and the diseases departed from them, and the evil spirits went out of them" (Acts 19:11–12).

Let's look at Peter's walk as he was led by the Holy Spirit:

> Inasmuch that they brought forth the sick into the streets, and laid them on beds and couches, that at the least the shadow of Peter passing by might overshadow some of them. There came also a multitude out of the cities round about unto Jerusalem being sick folks, and them which were vexed with unclean spirits: and they were healed every one.
>
> —ACTS 5:15–16

I have read many books on deliverance and I have yet to read one that gives the Holy Spirit recognition during deliverance. Neither have I read that the Holy Spirit causes demons to manifest in certain situations. He is the presence of God. As the Holy Spirit hovered over the earth, God spoke the Word—Jesus was the Word—and creation manifested (John 1:1).

Many times unclean spirits will manifest when I hug people because of the presence of the Holy Spirit. Simply touching them brings about the manifestation of unclean spirits. Often they will begin to weep, cough, and tremble.

The Holy Spirit enables us to walk with gifts of revelation. I shared these gifts with you earlier and how they operate for the kingdom of God and how they work against the kingdom of darkness. Just to refresh your memory they are word of knowledge, word of wisdom, and discerning of spirits.

The discerning of spirits is a gift of the Holy Spirit enabling a person to instantly discern between the Spirit of God and evil spirits. It is not human intelligence, experience, or ability. It is directly from God. It is not fortune telling. Satan and his demons can and will deceive the deliverance minister. "Now the Spirit speaketh expressly, that in the latter times some shall depart from the faith, giving heed to seducing spirits and doctrines of devils" (1 Tim. 4:1). If the minister has the gift of discerning spirits, he or she will know if unclean spirits are hiding. The Holy Spirit will give you revelation of the Spirit.

Sometimes you think you are done and the Holy Spirit will give you a word of knowledge. For example, a word of knowledge comes to you, in the case of rape, so you call for the spirit of perversion in the name of Jesus and set the person free. The Holy Spirit, Jesus, and you (the minister) are in partnership against the kingdom of darkness. You never want to minister deliverance without the Holy Spirit and Jesus. The Holy Spirit will give you revelation and power, and Jesus will give you the authority.

NOTES

INTRODUCTION

1. "Origin of Satan," Angelfire.com, www.angelfire.com/mi/dinosaurs/lucifer.html (accessed June 4, 2014).

CHAPTER 1
BACKGROUND ON DEMONS

1. Derek Prince, *God's Remedy for Rejection* (New Kensington, PA: Whitaker House, 1993), 27–27.

2. Basil Frasure, "The Wounded Heart," in *Bringing Every Thought Captive*, vol. 1 (San Angelo, TX: B. Frasure, 1996).

3. Ibid.

4. Ibid.

5. Ibid.

6. Ibid.

7. Ibid.

8. Kenneth E. Hagin, *Demons and How to Deal with Them*, vol. 2, Satan, Demons, and Demon Possession Series, 2nd ed. (Tulsa, OK: Faith Library Publications, 1987).

9. Kenneth E. Hagin, *The Holy Spirit and His Gifts* (Tulsa, OK: Faith Library Publications, 1987), 102.

10. Ibid., chap. 11.

11. Ibid., 102.

12. David Holt Boshart Jr , "Discerning of Spirits," Christ-Centered Mall, Inc., http://www.christcenteredmall.com/teachings/gifts/discernment.htm (accessed June 5, 2014).

13. Kenneth E. Hagin, *Ministering to the Oppressed* (Tulsa, OK: Faith Library Publications, 1978), 1.

14. Kenneth E. Hagin, *Discerning of Spirits* (Tulsa, OK: Faith Library Publications, n.d.), 1–3.

CHAPTER 2
METHODS OF DELIVERANCE

1.   Don Colbert, "The Cleansing Power of Forgiveness," Live Long Live Strong, LLC, 2008, http://www.livelong -livestrong.com/index.php?id=124 (accessed June 6, 2024).

2.   Ibid.

3.   Frank Hammond and Ida Mae Hammond, *A Manual for Children's Deliverance* (Kirkwood, MO: Impact Christian Books, 1996), 15–16.

4.   Bill Banks, *Deliverance for Children & Teens* (Kirkwood, MO: Impact Christian Books, 1989).

5.   Ibid.

6.   Ibid., 106–108.

7.   Frank Hammond and Ida Mae Hammond, *Pigs in the Parlor: The Practical Guide to Deliverance* (Kirkwood, MO: Impact Christian Books, 1973), 27.

8.   Ibid.

CHAPTER 4
THE DELIVERANCE MINISTER

1.   Hammond and Hammond, *Pigs in the Parlor*, 97.

2.   Ibid.

3.   Ibid.

4.   Hagin, *The Holy Spirit and His Gifts*, 121–122.

5.   Frasure.

6.   Hammond and Hammond, *A Manual for Children's Deliverance*, 21.

CHAPTER 5
STAYING FREE OF DEMONS

1.   Finis Dake, *Dake's Annotated Reference Bible* (Lawrenceville, GA: Dake Bible Sales, 1985), 212.

2.   Ibid., 214.

3.   Ibid.

4.   Ivory L. Hopkins, *Spiritual Warfare Training Manual* (Georgetown, DE: Pilgrim's Ministry of Deliverance, n.d.).

CHAPTER 6
HIERARCHY OF SATANIC SPIRITS

1. Kimberly Daniels, *Spiritual Warfare: How to Pray for Your City* (Jacksonville, FL: Spread the Word Publishing, 1999).
2. Michael Houdmann, "What Is Heaven Like," Got Questions Ministries, http://www.gotquestions.org/heaven-like.html (accessed June 7, 2014).
3. Dake, notes pg. 392.
4. Daniels, *Spiritual Warfare*.
5. Ibid.
6. Ibid.
7. Ibid.
8. Ivory L. Hopkins, *Deliverance from Christian Control Spirits* (Georgetown, DE: Pilgrim's Ministry of Deliverance, n.d.), 2.
9. Ibid., 1–2.
10. Ibid.
11. Ibid., 3, 6.
12. Ibid.

CHAPTER 7
HOLY SPIRIT: THE DELIVERER

1. Croft M. Pentz, *Outlines on the Holy Spirit* (Grand Rapids, MI: Baker Book House, 1978), 24.
2. Ibid., 60.

ABOUT THE AUTHOR

L OREATHA GUNNELS-MAYBERRY WAS born in Morrilton, Conway County, Arkansas. She was one of ten children of Matthew and Minnie Blackmon Gunnels, natives of South Carolina. Mr. Gunnels was a sharecropper, sawmill laborer, and railroad worker.

In her teens she moved to Kansas City, Missouri, and then later to Omaha, Nebraska, where she worked and attended school. She graduated from the University of Nebraska at Omaha in 1979 with a degree in criminal justice. While working on her master's degree in 1991, she received a higher calling. Loreatha answered the call of the Holy Spirit and became an ordained minister in 1996.

Loreatha is founder and executive director of Setting the Captives Free, an organization that is designed to rescue, restore, and release whole women and their children back into the community. God has given her grace in deliverance, healing the deaf, and healing of joints and bones.

God gave Loreatha the name Bethesda Worship and Deliverance Center. On November 1, 2008, Loreatha and her wonderful husband, Melvin Mayberry, who assists her in both endeavors, planted a church in Omaha, Nebraska, using the name that God had revealed to her.

The mother of five adult children, she currently ministers to the women at the Women's Correctional Center in York, Nebraska, in addition to speaking at various churches. She is also a part of other community organizations including North Omaha Village.

In 2007 Loreatha published her first book, a biographical sketch of her life from childhood through adulthood—*Beyond the Tears: From Misery to Joy.* Her hope is that this book, *Holy Spirit, The Deliverer,* will assist individuals of all ages in their quest for spiritual freedom by showing them how lives can be changed positively through ministering the way to receive deliverance and remain free of the demons that plague our lives.

CONTACT THE AUTHOR

The author may be contacted by email:
stcfree@cox.net